HOW TC
TO WOMEN

A Practical Guide on How to Eliminate Approach Anxiety,
Increase Your Social Confidence and Improve Your
Dating Life and Relationships

*The Only How-To-Approach-Women
Guide You Will Ever Need*

as Written by an Actual, Real, Live Woman

Table of Contents

Chapter 1

How to Develop a Personality That Attracts Women

"Nice guys" constantly whine that women only like douchebags. The sad truth is, the *actual* nice guys all seem to taken or gay.

If you're whining that you're a "nice guy," chances are, you aren't actually a nice guy. My childhood nerd is saddened by the fact that the jocks are now the actual nice guys and the nerds are the douchebags.

One word: Incels. The "involuntary celibates." The "loser virgins." Guess what? We don't owe you sex. We don't owe you politeness. We don't owe you kindness. We don't owe you a date or an explanation or fucking anything! Say it again for the back row!

WOMEN DON'T OWE MEN ANYTHING!

Know what I say to assholes who expect to get laid because they bought me dinner I didn't ask them to? "Thanks for dinner."

You don't want to buy us dinner, don't. But doing it doesn't mean you're gonna get laid. Listening to us cry, being there for us, helping us move—those are all awesome things to do. But you don't have to do any of it. You don't owe us anything. So if you choose to be kind, we thank you. Now get the fuck off our property, because we don't owe you sex. You wanna start charging us for your services, let us know when we ask you for help, what your hourly rate is, and remember: it's mostly illegal to pay in sex. Now, I personally, think brothels should be legal, but that's a subject for a different time.

Right now, we're working on developing a personality that attracts women. And Incels clearly don't. Don't be those guys.

But even if you're not calling yourself an Incel, you've done it, right? You've bought a woman dinner or helped her move or helped her with something and then expected to get laid, right? Or a makeout, at the very least.

This goes back to remembering that we're human beings. We're not vending machines where you put in enough kindness tokens and out pops sex.

We're living, breathing human beings, just like you. We have emotions, and yes, we may have more than you, but we have bad days that have nothing to do with our menstruation. I'm going to throw the proper words for things like that in here a bit so that by the end, hopefully you'll be more comfortable knowing they exist. If men were as disgusted by rape as they are by periods, rape would mostly cease to exist, because the men who are comfortable with women's periods and recognize it's not a choice and how the female body works are less likely to rape a woman. We'll get into consent later, because it's huge and neither men nor women are taught what it means.

Women are taught to go along to get along, to be people-pleasers, and that our value depends entirely on our looks. So, often, women don't say no. But they don't say yes either. They just try to ghost because they don't know if you're going to go psycho on them for rejecting them also. But I digress, and we will talk about why women ghost and all the inherent mixed signals we accidentally send later.

Back to the whole, "we're human beings" thing. I know, it's a crazy notion, but it totally works. Someone asked Joss Whedon how he manages to create such well-defined, strong female characters

2

(Buffy, Angel, Firefly). He said, "I've always thought women were, well, people."

Start viewing us as just people. Not goddesses who shouldn't talk to you, and certainly not sex objects who exist solely for your pleasure.

Many women may act like goddesses who shouldn't talk to you. Don't waste your time on them.

You may have it in your mind that you "deserve" a particular woman. Again, she's a human being. Look up the Thirteenth Amendment and the Emancipation Proclamation. No human is allowed to own another human in this country. That doesn't stop men from trying.

You don't "deserve" a woman. No matter how "nice" you are, she's not an object. She's not a toy in the claw machine that if you try hard enough, you'll get. She's a human being. She's either interested or she's not.

If she treats you poorly, she's not. But the bigger question is: why are you interested in her? Beauty fades. Crazy is forever. Pick your battles wisely.

Many women may act like sex objects whose sole desire is to please you. Many, many, many women. Because we've been taught that our entire value comes from men and if they find us sexually desirable, but we're not supposed to actually have sex with them.

When you're with these women, i.e. the majority of us, make sure she knows by your words and your body language that you *don't* need sex from her. We know you want it. Duh. But let her know that her *company* is why you're with her.

No matter what she's wearing, maintain eye contact. Actually, *listen* to her instead of waiting to talk or trying to fix the problem. She's not asking for advice or a handyman. She just wants a friend.

The second point the intro made was to back away when she's not interested. Books, movies, society—everyone may tell you to persist until you "get" her, or that you can treat her like shit if you have enough money. You can even "grab her by the pussy" without asking. Everyone who adheres to any of these philosophies is *wrong*. Look at the *type* of women they attract. There a lot of gold diggers who allow themselves to be treated like shit because he has money. The men who treat women like objects have a long list of complaints against them, either lodged formally or informally.

But women talk. You know this. So if you persist to one woman who said no repeatedly, she doesn't find your persistence "cute." She finds it crazy, stalker-ish, boy can't take a hint, dumbass asked me out again and I can only politely refuse him for so long before I go balls-out crazy on his ass- take your pick. We've used all these words and phrases in describing you to our friends. So, if you keep bugging one of us, you're out of luck with our friends too. This is the list of "informal" complaints. There may not be any lawsuits you have to talk or buy or charm your way out of, and it's still ridiculously easy to do so, but there are groups of women in your circles who wouldn't touch you with a ten-foot pole.

1.1 Personality Traits that Attract Women

In no particular order, I'm just throwing these out there. And who better qualified to write this list than a woman?

I don't purport to speak for all women. There are, of course, outliers who really *do* prefer douchebags. You'll find decent, not crazy women actually exist. We're usually just working. And I may find that decent, not perverted men actually exist, but they're probably just working. Or I don't notice when they hit on me. That happens too.

We'll go into deeper detail with each of these traits. We'll first start with the must-haves, then move to the must-not-haves. It may seem daunting and practically impossible. Don't worry; I'll walk you through it.

I may have been single long enough that I'm bitter and jaded and have a continual beef with the patriarchy. I'll own that. I'll give you a few insights deliberately as to why women think and do what they think and do. However, I've got the inside track here, and I didn't really start understanding us until my 30's. Thank the god I don't believe in I'm straight. I'll probably accidentally give you a few insights into the female brain too.

Having said that, really pay attention to this book. I'm going to write as I speak. I'm a no-nonsense, won't bullshit you, one of the guys' friends.

I can see what plagues men's minds about women, and hopefully give you an insight into what is so clearly a foreign alien species we need thirty thousand words, which may actually be longer than my master's thesis, which I counted in pages (157, btw).

Given all of that, you may pick up cues I don't deliberately lay down. But let me give you my qualifications as to why you should listen to me. One, as we've discussed, I'm a woman. Two, I do have a master's in exactly talking to humans. Yes, a basic human skill I still probably suck at. Communications is phony major. Lubcheko learn nothing. Three, I have no brothers, but I'm one of the guys. I'm the guy translator for my female friends.

When my female friends come to me with the "what did he mean when he said this?" bullshit, I answer them honestly. "Probably exactly what he said."

I don't know why women think men are so hard to figure out. The word "nothing" was slang in Shakespearean time to mean vagina. Kinda dehumanizing, but we get used to it. Point is, men are either

5

thinking about nothing, or…. nothing. We truly don't need hours of conversation detailing down to the color of your socks and if it had anything to do with her. Probably not. They were just somewhat clean. Hell, I have clean, somewhat clean, and dirty piles. I know exactly what's wearable by where on the floor it is.

I was actually also a jock in high school. I was a black belt and on the debate team. But no one really knew about the black belt thing because it wasn't through school. They just knew I beat the shit out bullies who picked on the nerds.

So, I'm about as butch as a straight woman can be. I always help the men out on Battle of the Sexes (I don't know why my niece gave me that game; I hate it. I *do*, however, know why she gave me a book about tips on having a gay ex-boyfriend. She's hilarious). I recognize this is a patriarchal society, and in that paradigm, women *must* learn the rules of men in order to survive, whereas, men don't have to learn the rules of women just to get a job or go on a date without the fear in the back of their mind that they could get raped.

So as much as I hate the patriarchy, I recognize we're all slaves to it. Have I used my boobs to get out of a speeding ticket a time or two? Of course, I have. Do I prop up the system I hate because I *can* use my body as currency? At times, yes. We're all guilty of adding to it. So yes, I hate it. Don't take it personally. I don't hate men. I hate the patriarchy. There's a difference. My father is the best man on the planet. For that, I will not tolerate the "he couldn't help it; he's a man" excuse.

Because I recognize the difference between individual men and the fucked-up system, I am qualified to tell you what women want and how we think. I also recognize the difference between individual women and the fucked-up system. I hope in reading this, you'll come to understand and appreciate those differences too. I hope in reading this, you'll learn to be able to talk to "that" woman- the one who's

6

the reason you clicked on this in the first place.

Remember she's a human being, and back off when she tells you to, and you'll be alright.

But let's start with the list of must-haves. This is by no means comprehensive, and it there are some outlier women. But developing these traits will not only help you talk to women, but help you succeed in life, and we'll delve deeper into each one accordingly.

Must-Haves:

- Confidence
- Intelligence
- Humor
- Kindness
- Humility
- Strong work ethic
- Socially adept
- Fiscally responsible
- Ability to adult
- Honesty
- Communication skills

Now let's look at a list of must-not-haves. You'll notice none of the must-haves are physical traits. Yes, there has to be chemistry and if she says looks don't matter, she's either lying or secretly means money does. But we're not talking about the vapid gold diggers. Wanna talk to them? Become a millionaire. That, I have no idea how to do, nor can I help you.

When *I* say looks don't matter, however, I'm not lying, and I'm not a gold digger. Looks *don't* matter to me. **My** looks don't matter. **You** still have to be pretty. I'm half kidding. I'm actually kidding, but I hate how that's the mindset men are trained to have- you'll notice 5's land 10's, but if she's an 8, she's out of luck unless she settles for a 2.

My point is, what I'm aiming to help you with is your personality. If there's no chemistry, there's no chemistry, and if you change yourself for her, you'll both hate you.

I also won't include bankruptcies or felonies on the must not have list. Those may not be turn-ons, but they're not personality traits. They can also become non-issues. Moving right along.

Must Not Haves (or Be)

- Arrogance
- Serial liar
- Serial Cheater
- Fake
- Perverted
- Obviously insecure
- Expect sex

Let's delve deeper into each trait. As stated, they're in no particular order. There's not a scale of importance. There probably is, but it will vary from woman to woman. Honesty is actually foremost important for me, but I forgot about until almost last because I still naively assume it's a given, even though I've been straight long enough to know it's not. Moving right along.

Confidence

What do you do well? It may be your boring job. Talk about work with confidence. Don't bore her, but inject humor, make fun of your boss or coworkers. Tell her how you ended up in that field and what you wanted to be when you were a kid. If talking about yourself is hard, listen to her. Ask probing questions, like what she does now and what she wanted to be as a kid.

Really listen. Maintain eye contact. Don't stare at her boobs. We're so sick of that. Don't think you're being subtle, either. We can tell. Don't check out other women. Again, you're not subtle. We can tell. Act as if you'd rather do nothing else in this world than listen to her. If you would rather be doing something else, she's probably not for you.

Use your manners. Don't talk with your mouth full, even if she does. But this is *on* the date. Let's talk about *getting* to the date.

When you ask her out, use the word date. I can count on one hand how many actual dates I've been on. Kinda depressing, actually.

"Would you like to go on a date with me?" Practice those words. If you met online, practice texting them to yourself.

If you just want to "meet up for coffee" or "hang out," she knows you think it's a date. But she probably isn't using that word when she tells her friends about it. To her, you're just another dude she's sifting through because you might become a friend or you might have hot friends or you'll help her move if she bats her eyelashes and still doesn't put out. Don't hate the player, bro. Hate the game.

Maybe I shouldn't be letting you in on the secrets of women. But if it creates more actual dates in this world, great! Make America date again. My stomach kinda hurt writing that play on words.

Give her a few options of when is best for it. Three specific dates. Let her choose one. Don't just say "whenever." That portrays either apathy or desperation.

If she says no or has an excuse for all three dates (remember, we ghost- more on that later), be gracious about. Say okay. Don't call her names. Don't tell her she was too fat for you anyway and you were doing her a favor by asking her out. Remember women talk. You have no idea who our friends are. Or their friends.

And **don't** ask why not. The simple answer is, she's not interested. Why isn't she interested? Does it matter? She's just not. She's not gonna be if you change yourself to please her. She doesn't owe you an explanation. She's just not interested. Move on. You don't deserve her. She's not an object. Just move on. Thank her for not leading you on.

Don't offer to still be friends. Not at this stage in the game. We know what you're doing. You're playing the "friends until I can get in her pants" game. She might say yes, but she doesn't mean it. She won't call or text and she'll conveniently forget who you are if you do.

Now if *she* offers to be friends, say yes. Mean it. Say yes when she invites you out with her mates, even if one of them is her new boyfriend. Call or text. Invite her to hang out with you *and* your buddies if you're doing something more exciting than playing video games unless she's a gamer too. **Don't** play the "friends until I can get in her pants" game. We know what you're doing.

Okay, so she's either said yes or no, and you were gracious if she said no. So, let's move on to her saying yes. Don't ask if she's sure or thank her for saying yes. You sound desperate.

She's said yes. Awesome! What's the next thing out of your mouth? "So, what do you want to do?"

Nope! Nopity nope nope! She's already bored! Plan it! Plan something she'll remember. Actually, *read* her profile if you met online. What are her interests? If you met online, suggest you meet at the place of the date. If she wants a ride, she'll ask. Most women feel safer meeting a stranger in public. This is a world man don't know. We're afraid to say yes, we're afraid to say no; it's not paranoia. It's just life. She'll feel safer if you suggest to meet her there.

You know her in real life, but not well enough to know her interests? Still don't ask her what she wants to do. Plan it. Make it somewhat out of the ordinary, like the aquarium or the zoo or a museum. Make yourself memorable. If you make her plan it, she'll probably suggest a dinner and a movie so she doesn't have to talk to you much, or just dinner or just a movie. She's already bored.

Okay, the date's a few days away. Go ahead and send good morning and good night texts. That's cute. Don't ask for nudes. Seriously. Don't. If she wants you to see her naked, she'll send you some. Never gotten unsolicited titty pics? No, I didn't think so. On that note, don't **ever, ever, ever** send unsolicited dick pics. Don't "count down" in texts to her. Again, it looks desperate. And don't make any insinuations about getting laid, or ask if she's a virgin or tell raunchy jokes. Now you're just like every other douchebag out there.

Making yourself memorable in a good way makes dating more exciting for her and less of a chore. If she's excited to date you, don't you already have more confidence?

Intelligence

You don't have to be Stephen Hawking. Some women don't even care about science. But you really do have to be able to string words together to make a coherent sentence, and then do that a few times to have an actual conversation.

There are some actual real setbacks to this that have nothing to do with intelligence. English isn't your first language, you have autism or have had a traumatic brain injury, for example. These are things she'll need to know before the date. If they're a deal breaker for her, her loss. Seriously. But don't say that. Be gracious. Don't use those as excuses to not try to ameliorate your life or improve yourself in any manner. Just let her know that it may take you longer to answer a question, or your words might come out backwards or something.

11

Intelligence and education are not the same thing. I had a few real dumbass professors, and some high school dropouts are quite smart.

But you're smart in *something*. Hopefully, you have a few common interests so what you're smart in doesn't bore her. If you don't have any common interests, move on. Again, beauty fades. Crazy is forever. Pick your battles wisely.

Humor

Everyone has different styles of humor. If your humor tends to be toward rape jokes, don't do it. It's not funny when we don't know you. It's scary, actually.

Once I was the only female at a party and the dude next to me kept telling me rape jokes. I'm not amused. Yeah, I'm big and strong and a black belt, and I wasn't disabled then. But you don't get to choose your reaction. Your brain chooses fight, flight, or freeze. *You* don't. And if your brain chooses fight? There's still a good chance he's got us beat on upper body strength, especially if there are six of them and they think it's just funny and we need to "chill out." So, I made up an excuse and said I was tired and needed to leave. Dude asked if I was safe to drive sleepy. I said I was safer to drive sleepy than stay there. He looked offended like he might joke about that shit, but he'd never *do* it!

We don't know that. Most rapes happen by people the victim knows. Many rapists *and* victims don't understand consent. Unless you *know* her, and you *know* she'll find it funny, don't go there.

Also, don't do racist or homophobic or any of that humor. Not until you know her and that she'll find it funny, or if you're playing Cards Against Humanity, where everybody knows you're *actually* kidding.

But everyone has different styles of humor. If she doesn't laugh at your jokes, it's not because she didn't get them. It's because they weren't funny. **Don't** explain them like she's an idiot. Self-deprecating humor rarely fails. Especially if your joke just did.

"Sorry. That was my dad's joke. Not one of his best. Wait it was his best. He's a lawyer."

Again, hopefully, you have some common ground that you can both find amusing.

Kindness

If you open her door and pull out her chair but treat the server like shit, she notices. If you flirt incessantly with the server, she notices that too. If you take the parking spot from someone who signaled for it or park in a handicap spot or ditch her all night, she notices all of that. Just don't be a dick. Not to her, not to the server, not to other people. I mean sure, if someone tries to kill you, you try to kill 'em right back. But in general, don't be a dick.

Be courteous. Don't spend the whole evening texting or checking the score of the game or talking about yourself. You know how you've felt on bad dates or when someone you don't like is trying to talk to you. Don't make her feel like that. Just think to yourself, "am I treating her the way I'd like to be treated?" If that doesn't work for you, think "Am I treating her the way I'd want suitors to treat my daughter or niece or future one?" If the answer is no, treat her better, stat.

If you're talking shit about everyone you know, she wonders what you're saying about her. If "all" your exes were crazy, she's guessing what the common denominator was. In fact, don't talk about your exes. If she is, she's probably just nervous. We get nervous too.

Humility

Admit when you make a mistake. Own it and move on. Be gracious if she rejects you. Don't tell her she was too fat for you anyway, or act like you were doing her a favor by wanting to bang her. We can get meaningless sex without trying. It's the meaning that's harder to come by.

Humility doesn't mean hate yourself. It doesn't mean insecurity. It just means admit where you're weak. Admit where you're human. Accept rejection graciously. Apologize when you screw up. Just own your shit. You look better, you have less to hide, and you sound better when she talks about you, which she will, good or bad.

Strong Work Ethic

The economy sucks. Let's not beat around the bush here. You're probably ridiculously overqualified for your job, and so is she. The older Gen-X's and the Boomers are holding onto their jobs forever.

But having a shitty job and maybe even hating it doesn't mean you do it poorly. You do it well. You might be continuing to look, but you keep doing your job well.

Being responsible at your job spills over into every aspect of your life. You're more likely to be punctual in your social life, which is a mark of courtesy. You're more likely to squeak by with enough tact to live among other humans if you can do it at work. Then it's easier to implement that in your social life. You're more likely to be all around responsible and have goals if you have a strong work ethic.

It doesn't matter what your job is or how much you make if you have goals. Having goals is sexy. Having achievable goals is sexy. Sure, tell her about how you want to become a movie star somehow—they're bound to discover you at McDonald's someday, right? But achievable goals, ambitions, motivations, and accomplishments are all sexy.

Socially Adept

We're not asking for Prince Charming. He's a serial cheater anyway, and not the least bit sincere. We're not even asking for charming. Ted Bundy was.

We're asking for you to be able to adapt to social situations. If we run into our parents, it will most likely be more awkward for us. Just adapt. Roll with it. Be polite. Roll with whatever title she introduces you as, unless she drops "boyfriend" without discussion. But friend, gay friend, roommate's boyfriend- roll with any of those. If you run into your ex, it'll be awkward. If you drop "girlfriend" without discussion, she might roll with it because it's your ex. She might do that to you if she runs into hers. Just adapt.

What if she has an out and out, full on panic attack, the kind where she can't breathe and you think she's going to die? Don't tell her to calm down. Just hold her hand and tell her to breathe slowly.

But that's not likely. The point is, you may meet her friends at some point. You may run into each other's families or exes. You might be awkward. Hell, my friends tell me how awkward I am all the time. And I further exacerbate the embarrassing moments by doing really stupid shit. I just responded to myself on a guy's dating profile because I thought he'd said it. I thought he was so witty and clever too! Welp, I won't be hearing from him ever. So, I make fun of myself because it's actually pretty hilarious, and move on.

That's what I mean by adapt and roll with it. Own it and move on. It's okay to make fun of yourself. It's probably even okay to make fun of her or her friends if they totally walked into it. If you have to reach for it, don't do it.

You get to the restaurant and you no longer have a reservation because someone screwed up their job. Don't yell at them. We all make mistakes. Ask for a manager, ask for a gift card for your troubles because you have to go somewhere else tonight, but you'd love to come here some night. Be polite about it. They might say no. Doesn't hurt to ask. Either way, just roll with it. Stay calm. That's socially adept. Are you gonna be socially awkward at times? Who isn't? But just calmly roll with unexpected situations.

Fiscally Responsible

It doesn't matter how much you make, spend it wisely. Whatever your living situation is, be responsible about it. No one likes a mooch. If you ask her if you can borrow $20 three dates in—or one—she's gonna nope the fuck right out of there.

But in whatever year you're reading this, she may make more than you. It isn't fair that you should be expected to spot every date. If you get to a steady relationship, discuss that with her.

Until then, plan dates you can afford. And no, I'm not talking Netflix and chill. Again, we don't even have to try. Know why? Boobs. Now you're not paying attention to anything else in this book because I said boobs. Menstruation. Did that bring you back? Plan picnics. Plan stargazing or people watching, and making up stories about strangers. Cook a meal together (clean your place first).

Bottom line: if you can't afford it, don't do it. If you want to impress her with gifts, spend some time at the dollar store finding things she'd like. Buy a single rose.

If you're fiscally responsible, she sees that you're long-term material.

Ability to Adult

Having a strong work ethic, being socially adept, being fiscally responsible—these are all part of *adulting*. If your living situation is that you still live with your parents, make sure you're helping out around the house, and hopefully paying rent. Change your oil, feed your pets, learn to cook, and clean as you go so it's not overwhelming.

Just be an adult. Get to where you don't *need* a relationship or even sex. You're with her because you enjoy her company. Period.

Honesty

I really should've put this first, but my naive brain thinks it's just a given, even though I've been a straight woman long enough to know it's not.

She doesn't need to know every detail of your life. But if you have a wife or girlfriend, she *does* need to know that. If women are so crazy, why do men insist on having more than one? Did it ever occur to them that it's *this* very behavior that drives us crazy?

Just be honest. Tell her if you have a girlfriend. If you have to lie about your relationship with her, it's not a healthy relationship. If you think you have to lie to *get* her, remember two things: she's a human being, not an object, and back off if it's not working.

Don't borrow your neighbor's kid to impress her. If you need to borrow your neighbor's kid, make it so you can go to a kids' movie without looking like a creeper; not to impress a woman. If it does, though, admit the kid isn't yours.

If you lie about your job or your income or anything, eventually the truth will ouch. I mean out. And someone who would like you exactly as you are is now missing out because you're pretending to be someone else.

It's okay to disagree with her. It's okay to call her out on her bullshit. It's okay if she calls you out. She doesn't want a carbon copy of herself. If she hates pickles, it's okay if you still like them. You don't need to apologize or justify or change your behavior.

Be whoever the hell makes you happy to be. If she doesn't like that person, someone else will. Or not. Maybe you'll die alone. But you have to live with yourself the rest of your life. Make sure you like that person. If you do, you won't settle for someone who's "settling" for you.

Keep your own opinions and views and likes and dislikes. If you make fun of communication majors for having a phony major then find out she's a comm major, own it. Be honest. Maybe just a shrug. But don't backtrack now. It *is* a phony major. Lubcheko learn nothing.

Communication Skills

Texting once a week, "sup?" isn't going to keep her attention. Text good morning and good night. Ask how her day was. Actually *listen*. Don't rush in to fix problems. Tell her what's going on in your mind. If you're legit too busy to text her for a while, say that when you do. "Hey I was busy. What's up?" We over analyze shit to death. I wish we didn't. Especially English majors, which was my other major. I mean, we spend 20 minutes discussing what the word *the* meant in a poem. We're ridiculous.

If she's the type who expects an immediate response and you just can't do that, let her know early on. If you expect an immediate response and she just can't do that, accept it.

••••••

Okay, so we've discussed the must-haves that women want. Again, it's not a comprehensive list, and I can't speak for all women. But the goal here is an actual relationship, amirite?

If the goal is just sex, there are plenty of horny, desperate women. If the goal is an actual relationship, that's a lot harder to come by.

Many women want a relationship, but we're sick of sifting through the haystacks for the needles. We're sick of sifting through the men who only want sex for the long-term minded ones. We're sick of all the "Wanna fuck?" messages in our inboxes.

Remember the two rules: treat us like we're human beings and back away when it's not working.

"Wanna fuck?" is far from a stellar line and comes across as thinking of us as just sex objects.

Seriously, this whole book could be summed up in the intro. But I'm actually writing it for you. Plus, I've added an extra chapter: Why Women Do the Crazy Things They Do. You're welcome.

But moving right along to the must not have personality traits.

Arrogance

This goes with the humility factor. Hot douchebags know they're hot, so they're cocky. If that's you, stop. But it probably isn't you. The kind of arrogance a normal to fugly looking dude has is anger at being rejected. You'd think the fugly ones would be used to it.

Here's the thing: it's actually scary rejecting a dude because we see all the time on the news about women who got killed when they said no. I'm really hoping that's not you either.

So, you're probably in the middle. And you might call her names if she rejects you. Don't. Just move on.

But arrogance isn't only about not handling rejection. It's a numbers game. We know this. And some women will give men their numbers out of politeness or because the writer in them wonders where the story will go (a part of me wants to kill that writer, but it's the only thing that keeps me somewhat sane).

Arrogance is also about chatting up every single woman you see until one of them gives you her number. Listen up, Boomhauer, this is why you're striking out: if you're doing it online, message them individually. If you chat with all of them on the group page, none of them feel special because you're flirting with Every. Single. One.

Even if you're flirting with them in DM's (and ask permission before just sending them one), we talk. You know this. I hate that I contribute to the stereotype of gossipy girl (and you've noticed I haven't said 'girl' yet. We're women. Get used to using that word. Or chick.), but really, we talk. You know this. But your odds are still better if you're the type to hit on everyone in a skirt if you do it in private messages.

But really, ease up on the hitting on everyone. "But beggars can't be choosers," you might whine. Okay- let me repeat this: humility is not hating yourself. Humility is just not thinking about yourself all the time, either in a negative or positive light. So, thinking you have to beg for a date? That's not being humble. It's *still* being arrogant. Because you're *still* thinking about *yourself* all the time.

So, find a type. Okay, you might say. Jennifer Lawrence, but like, my religion (or college major or insert whatever is your personal top must have). Dude. If she exists, she ain't going for you. Again, with the arrogance, thinking either you have to beg for a date or you "deserve" a freaking goddess. Dude. No. Just no.

Another common type of arrogance men have is assuming women are dumb. Mansplaining is when a man explains something to a woman that she knows *very* well. Men explained papers to me in grad school because they didn't think I understood what the author was saying. Papers *I* wrote. I *was* the author. And yet, I needed a big strong man to tell me what it really meant because a woman couldn't have had a good understanding of The Simpsons or Eminem.

Don't be that guy. If she says she likes sports, don't "test" her knowledge. Take her word for it. If she says she likes cars, just believe her. If she's lying to impress you, the truth will eventually out. But most likely, she actually likes sports and cars. I actually like Simpsons and Eminem. Not all women are the same, just like not all men are the same.

So now we've defined the types of arrogance most men are guilty of having. Don't be that guy. Next.

Serial Liar

This one's huge. Find me a dude who doesn't lie and I'll find you a sane woman. Actually, I know plenty of sane women.

There's really just one thing to say about this subject.

DON'T EVER FUCKING LIE TO US!!!!!!!!!

Yes, that sentence required an expletive. Why do you think we won't find out? Why do you think we believe you? We're not actually as dumb as you seem to think we are. We just know it's pointless to argue the point.

If you ever find a woman who calls you out on your bullshit, don't ever let her go. She's a gem.

What do you gain from lying? Don't tell her you'll call her if you have no intention of calling her. **DON'T** tell her you love her just to get in her pants. Dick move. Now she's fallen for you, and all her friends hate you now too. Even if you get your shit together and come back around and *actually* love her a few months later, all her friends still hate you. Friends hold grudges longer than scorned women. Maybe because we're sick of hearing about your shit and we've been telling her you're a no good liar from the beginning! But I've also been the scorned woman. My friends still hate them.

Sex? Is that it? Is that what you get from lying? Was it worth fucking up someone for? You couldn't find a horny chick on Tinder who's been hurt so much she has no heart left? Or you weren't good looking enough for her, so you lied to someone who kinda liked you until she loved you? Fuck you, man. Don't be that guy.

Okay, so you're not that dude. What are you lying about? You were studying with a female friend you think is kinda cute, but can't say it, so you were studying with "Jared"? Dude, just tell us. So, you still have female friends. Awesome. Maybe don't tell us you think she's kinda cute. Not lying doesn't mean tell us *everything,* it just means don't lie.

We get that men lie and cheat (that's next). Maybe that's what drives us crazy. If you could **not** do that, that'd be great. It really would put you above 98 percent of every other dude out there.

Is she still crazy? If you actually love her, you can help her out. If she loves you, she'll help you. Get this: it's okay for men to feel something besides anger. It's okay for men to be depressed. It's okay not to be okay. It doesn't make you less of a man. Because she's probably not crazy. I keep using that word because it's the stereotype. They're timesavers, right? Okay, they're not. But men tend to understand the catch-all word "crazy" better than words like depression, anxiety, stress, etc., so I'm using it.

But listen up: we're not actually crazy, no matter how much I will continue to use that word. And you don't have to repress your emotions. You don't have to lie about them either. If you actually try to communicate with her, it'll probably go better than you expect.

Serial Cheater

This goes hand-in-hand with the serial liar one. I've said it before, but I'll say it again: if we're so crazy, why do you want more than one of us?

This is another reason we're guarded. This is another reason we don't trust you. You're not our ex, we know that. But so many of them did, we have to wonder what's wrong with *us*? It drains the self-esteem, it really does. Whether we're being cheated on or cheated with, he's still lying and cheating, and we always find out, even if we don't confront them.

We're not the legal system. You're not innocent until proven guilty. And the legal system is plenty flawed too. We *want* to trust you. We've fallen victim to believing men just because we *wanted* to, even though it wasn't logical to do so.

Don't cheat. Break up with us first. It's better for everyone in the long run. It's that simple.

Fake

No one likes fake people. My coworkers used to ask me how come I made such better tips than they did. I said it was because I kept the customers' drinks full, I pre-bussed my tables, and I wasn't fake. None of this "How are we today?" falsetto voice bullshit. None of this "Everything's my favorite!" nonsense. I was like, "Hey, what can I get ya?" and "No, you don't want the pot roast." Of course, my coworkers said customers couldn't tell they were fake, and I got my good tips from my boobs. Fine. Don't take my advice. I'll keep making more than you.

The customers could tell when they were being fake. Everyone can tell. And now that I'm in a wheelchair, *everyone's* fake to me.

But it's not just the tone of voice- the overly polite, higher pitch than normal, condescending tone. It's also pretending to like her interests if you don't. We touched on this in Confidence.

If you don't actually like Gilmore Girls, don't pretend you do. If you're watching it with her just to be with her, but you actually hate it.... that's really cute. Tell her that. Be honest. Be real. Be orange in a sea of gray.

Yes, it's cliché to say "be yourself." But really, who else are you gonna be? Just be the best version of yourself you can be.

Perverted

This is huge. Know what the difference between a nice guy and a pervert? Timing. They all say the same things. They all want sex. They all want butt stuff. But if you start off with that shit, you're a pervert.

If you wait until you've developed an actual rapport, a real friendship with potential, then it's appropriate to say dirty things. She might even think it's cute.

Friends with potential is not even close to FWB. Friends with potential is what most women want. An actual, real friendship that has the potential to grow into something more. But you may move faster physically than she wants, and she may move faster emotionally. If you can develop the actual friendship first, move physically at her pace and let her know she might need to slow down emotionally.

Then you can say all the perverted things you've been holding back. Maybe not all. But really, the only difference is timing.

Wait until it's appropriate to be a pervert, and then you're not a pervert!

Obviously Insecure

When you thank us for saying hi to you, you reek of desperation.

When you can't make eye contact or speak above a whisper to save your life, we know you haven't spoken to a real, live woman in a while.

You don't need to be charming and suave. Again, Ted Bundy, but you do need to be able to carry on a conversation without us wondering if you're going to wet your pants.

You're nervous. We get that. We get nervous too. Back to confidence. Tell yourself you're amazing every day in the mirror. Cheesy, I know. But there's a difference between a little nervous and obviously insecure.

This lends itself to being socially awkward to a fault. Being a little socially awkward is normal, maybe even kinda cute. I think my social awkwardness is adorable. I'd date the hell out of myself! And I do!

But when you're ridiculously socially awkward, it's just embarrassing. This can show itself by a display of macho arrogance, being a douche to everyone, or trying to become the invisible wallflower.

Notice how your behavior changes when a woman is present. Do you tend toward either of those extremes? Take note and make a conscious effort to tone it down or engage in conversation when it happens.

Expect Sex

We know you want it. Guess what? We do too. We just want to be treated like a human being first. We're more than tits and ass.

We don't owe you anything. You don't owe us anything. We use you, you use us. This is the game. If you don't want to help us when we "need" you, don't.

Here's a little insight into the female brain: men seem to like the archaic and misogynistic notion of the "damsel in distress," so they often "need" men when they really don't. I can't possibly be the only straight woman who can kill a spider.

So, many women use men because they can. I've been left watching movies alone on my couch many times because a girl texted him, needing him, and I didn't need him; I was okay. Yes, I used the word girl. Those who do that are girls. This book is about how to talk to women. But I *did* need him. I needed him to just watch a movie with me, be my friend, give me social interaction. Just because I don't need you to fix stuff doesn't mean I don't need you. Pay attention to those women, the non-needy ones. You don't have to rush off to help a damsel in distress and leave the warrior because she doesn't "need" you. You don't have to fix shit because a female text you.

So... don't do it. Unless you actually want to, without expecting anything in return.

1.2 How to Beat Insecurity and Neediness

It's hard to develop confidence. Men have expectations and body shaming too. Men have feelings and emotions too. They're just told to hide them. So, more men die from suicide every year than women. Really don't be that guy. If you've read this far, you're trying to be a better dude. I applaud you. The world needs more of you.

So how are you gonna develop confidence? Let's take a few pointers.

Tell yourself you're great.

I know it's cheesy. I really do. But it helps. It really does. Do it every day. Find something you like about your body and your mind.

Is anxiety an issue for you? Who am I kidding? Of course, it is. If you have extreme, crippling anxiety, name it after a fictional character you hate. A real one will cause you more. Then tell it to go to hell. You're smart and logical. Your anxiety isn't. It helps to separate yourself from it.

But let's talk about normal, talking to women anxiety. Your palms are sweaty, your voice magically raised and you feel thirteen again, you triple check your fly and stumble over your feet. Let's go back to the basics.

1. Remember she's a human being. Not a goddess, and not a sex object. Human, just like you.

2. Back off when she says to. Respect her boundaries.

Okay, those are really the only two things you need to know. That's why they're on repeat. But let's go back to more intro basics.

- Make eye contact.

- Smile.

- Say, "Hi. How are you?"

Chances are, she'll smile back and answer the question, even if she's only doing it to be polite. But striking up conversations with women is great practice to overcome your insecurity.

Let's talk neediness now.

Are you calling every hour? Don't. Are you offering to do anything for her, fix everything for her, take care of her all the time? That screams desperate and needy.

Do you keep asking her for a blowjob after she's said no? Do you even go so far as to offer to eat her out in return? Why do men beg for sex? Why do they think their penis is magical and will cure multiple sclerosis or whatever chronic illness they have (that one's at the top of my list)? You're being needy *and* perverted *and* breaking the two cardinal rules simultaneously. Well done, slick.

Whether you're calling her all the time or begging for sex or getting impatient when she takes some time to respond to a text because she has a life, or trying to convince her to blow off her friends and kick it with you—anything you're begging for (it's not cute persistence, it's annoying as fuck neediness), you reek of desperation. You reek of neediness. You need her to need you. You want her to want you. Feel free to break out into song.

So how do you overcome that? Remember the cardinal rules. She's human, and back off. But let's be a little more specific.

- Recognize she has a life outside of you. Respect that. Don't send angry, "why haven't you responded?" texts. Give her space. Then let her *choose* to share it with you.

- Develop your own hobbies, apart from her, so you're not staring at your phone all day, waiting for her.

- **Don't** try to play games. This whole dating bullshit *is* a game, and it sucks. But don't deliberately wait to text her back. But also, don't immediately text her and send her like 12. Needy.

- **Don't** thank her for responding. She's not a goddess; she's human.

- **Do** use self-deprecating humor. Don't make it sound like you hate yourself. I've mentioned a few times how adorably awkward I am. Stuff like that. Why is a straight woman giving advice on how to get the ladies? Because I get hit on by a woman at least once a week and propositioned by a couple at least once a month. I'm strickly dickly, so no thank you, but I'm flattered by the offer. My point is, I get the ladies without trying. So, listen up, fellas. And I get the men who just want to bang me. Not flattered, no thank you. And I get decent men, but my subconscious hates me, so I don't realize they're hitting on me until the moment's passed.

- **Do** back off when she says it. Here's the rub about that: women are so inherently trained to not straight out reject a guy because he might go psycho on her, and men just **don't** get hints. So, they're talking past each other the whole time. She says, "I don't need anything, I'm good, thanks." He hears, "I don't need that specific thing you offered." So he tries again. Rinse and repeat. *Listen* to the words women actually say. They often do mean exactly what they say, but they just had to say it really politely. By the time they've said it politely a few times, they say it not politely. Then she's a "crazy bitch." Calling her names also screams neediness.

- **Do** walk with your head held high. She's not better than you, but it is her right not to choose you.

- **Don't** look down your nose women just to "look cool" or "get them to notice you." You're not better than them, but it is your right not to choose them.

- **Don't** invite yourself over to her place or out with her friends unless you're already legit friends. Looks desperate to be in her company. If she says you'd be bored if you do invite yourself along, what she means is, "I really don't want you there."

1.3 Why Your Mindset is Crucial

You have to believe you're capable of talking to women. We're not mystical creatures; we're human beings. I keep repeating myself because we're so rarely portrayed that way, and men so rarely view us as such. They think we're obstacles, blocking sex. Nah, bro, you got your hand, if that's all we are. You gotta remember she's a human. Keep telling yourself that so it'll be easier to talk to her.

We have anxiety too. We don't know what to say on first dates either. We get scared of commitment sometimes too. Some women are terrified of it. Sometimes we just want a fuck too. We're really not that different from you.

So, your mindset is, "Okay, she's just another person. Like Brad or John or my math teacher. But I don't want to bang them. But right now, I gotta focus. Focus on just *talking* to her. Don't think about banging."

Am I doing a pretty good job of getting in the male brain? I'm one of the guys. But I have boobs. So I'm like a secret spy in both camps, a double-double agent. I spy on both camps. I report to both camps. Both camps love and hate me. And all the camps in between. I traverse those passages. I'm a huge LGBT ally. I spy on everyone and report to everyone. I'm universally admired and hated. It's a gift.

But seriously, don't be one-track-minded here. Focus on just *talking* to her.

Mindset traits necessary for approaching women:

- Confidence. You got this.

- Positive affirmation. You've been telling yourself you can do this for so long, you might actually believe yourself.

- Humility. Not backing off looks needy and desperate.

- Focus. You're going to actually *listen* to her.

Most of all, you gotta know what you bring to the table. If you don't think you bring anything, ask your mom. Ask your friends. Ask yourself. Figure out what you bring to the table. Once you know that, you have that positive mindset, that knowledge that you have something to offer another human being in a conversation. That's power. When you falter, when you feel nervous, bring your attention back to whatever it is you can easily talk about.

Your mindset is all about positivity and confidence. She's just another person. Instead of being intimidated by intelligent women, be enlightened by them. Let them teach you something. In doing that, I promise you'll discover something you can teach her.

1.4 Do as Much as You Can to Improve

Give yourself positive affirmations every day. Make goals. Make a budget. Learn a new skill. Start adulting better- cooking, cleaning, personal hygiene. Make your appearance and your home so that you wouldn't be embarrassed if she suddenly dropped by. "She" as in, whoever that woman is you haven't gotten up the courage to talk to, who made you want to click on this book.

Exercise, read, and make new friends. Be the kind of person *you* would want to date.

1.5 Practice, Practice, Practice

Start making small talk with strangers, male and female. Again, make eye contact. Smile. Say, "Hi. How are you?"

The more comfortable you get making small talk with strangers, the easier normal conversation becomes.

Chapter 2

How to Approach Women

Back to the basics. Make eye contact. Smile. Say, "Hi. How are you?"

2.1 How to Overcome Approach Anxiety with this Simple Trick (the 3-second rule)

Say hi within three seconds of approaching her before your anxiety (remember, name it and tell it to go to hell) tells you that you suck.

Don't get close to her at the bar or near the chips, or wherever, hoping she'll say something first. Your anxiety is lying to you the longer you stand there, staring at her like a creeper. Remember, you guys aren't very good at being subtle. We know when you're checking us out. Unless you're ridiculously hot and you're checking *me* out. I tend to miss those moments.

When you approach her, say hi within the first three seconds. Eye contact. Smile. "Hi. How are you?"

Pick-up lines don't work on the average woman because we've heard them all. Stick with the basics.

And remember, your anxiety is lying to you. You do not suck. You are not worthless.

Even if she rejects you, you still have a lot to offer someone else. But don't hit on every woman at the party. That makes us feel less special. But simply talking to everyone at a party makes you social, so be sure to throw in approaching a few men too, to shake things up and look social as opposed to desperate.

2.2 Three Ways to Start a Conversation

Again, back to the basics. "Hi. How are you?" After you've got that going, here are a few open-ended conversation points to use.

2.2.1 Opinion Openers

Ask her opinion about broad social trends or topics to start with, but avoid religion or politics. It's really difficult to stay abreast of current events without discussing politics, but it is possible. Here are a few suggestions. Asking favorites is usually safe. You might try to reword it so it doesn't sound like an interrogation. If she gives one-word answers to follow up questions, she's not interested. Back away, not today. Sure, keep talking to her, but don't ask for her number, don't ask her out. Just be social.

Be prepared to answer the same questions you ask.

- What's your favorite TV show?

Follow-ups work better if you like it too. Yeah? Best episode ever? Who would you marry, kill, and fuck from that show (Don't get jealous: the marry, kill, fuck game is fun with any group—work, TV shows, books, etc.)? How do you think the writing could be improved?

- What character do you find the most relatable?

That question can be substituted for movie, book, TV show that's gone off the air, non-American show, or play or video game, but expect weird looks from those last two.

- What did you want to be when you were 17?

Follow-up: How far away are you from that? Are you happy with the distance or is it spot on? Are you happy with that? (Side note: when I taught public speaking, I made my students give impromptus every week. This one was always around midterms. It created BFFs in the room. The whole class. The younger students and non-trads also became close).

- Are you a cat person, a dog person, or a pig person?

Follow-ups: Did you know a pig's penis extends to 18 inches and rotates like a corkscrew and the female pig can hold an orgasm for half an hour? We should worship these creatures instead of eat them! But they're so tasty!

Okay, do not use those as follow-ups! I'm totally kidding! I mean, the facts are true, but do NOT say them to a woman you don't know! Again, the difference between a nice guy and a pervert is timing. Fine, I'm a pervert. The secret is out. I just threw a pig in there because I just found out my friend has a 200-pound pet pig. But throwing that in there will be unique. It can be substituted out for a ferret, sloth, porcupine, skunk, lizard, or any non-normal pet. Have an interesting story or fun fact or friend who has one of these pets, or have one yourself. You're still thinking about that 18-inch penis, aren't you? It's okay; I'm still thinking about that half-an-hour-long orgasm.

- What was your favorite subject in school?

Follow-ups: What was your least favorite? Did you go to college? How did those affect your college major? What classes did you find useless pertaining to your major? How do you think the education system could be improved?

- What was your favorite Christmas gift ever?

Follow-ups: Who gave it to you? What was your least favorite? What was the best gift you've given? (Christmas can be substituted for any gift-giving holiday or birthday). Do you and your friends randomly give gifts to each other? What was that favorite? Least favorite? (Side note: least favorite gifts can be funny stories. Like the time my mom gave me a case of Slim Fast for my birthday. Good times. And really listen to favorites in case it does turn into a relationship).

- What fictional character do you relate to best?

Follow-ups: What do you have in common with them? What fictional character would you like to be like?

- Have you ever broken any bones or stayed overnight in the hospital?

Follow-ups: What's the best injury story you've heard?

Okay, I hope I've given you enough ideas to be able to start conversations and to come up with ideas on your own.

2.3 How to Make a Great First Impression

Remember how to approach anyone? We're using it again. 1. Eye contact. 2. Smile. 3. Say "Hi. How are you?"

Using a lame line doesn't stand out. Those opinion openers I gave you- that makes you stand out. Here's another helpful hint. Most cheesy romcoms are written by men as well, so they have no idea how real women would respond to the cheesy lines they use in the movies.

<<Insert Robert Downey, Jr. sigh gif here>>

Okay, so you've approached her within three seconds (I'll agree with that one), using the four magic words I've repeated a lot. You haven't looked below the neck **at all** (because you're not subtle. Just know that), or commented on her looks.

Now say something she'll remember. Again, the openers I had are original. Or ask her what superpower she'd have if she was a superhero or a supervillain. **Don't** hit on her. You're not playing hard to get, you're not playing games; you're just not competing for her attention.

Have a great conversation. Really *listen* to her. Don't allude to sex **at all**. Seriously. **At all.** Again, the difference between a nice guy and a pervert is timing. Most are perverts. If you can have a conversation with her without looking at her boobs, her ass, her legs- anything below the neck, and **not** make any sexual innuendos, even if she does (but it's okay to laugh), you're already above 98 percent of all the other men.

2.4 Why the Way You Talk is More Important Than What You Talk About (Body Language Basics)

Let's take some tips from pop culture. Are you a close talker from Seinfeld? Are you a leaner, from While You Were Sleeping? It may be clear I stopped watching tv and new movies a while ago, although I do plan to see Bohemian Rhapsody. That's been my karaoke jam for 20 years.

But don't close talk. Don't lean. Don't hyper-focus on us. Eye contact, yeah, but still blink like a normal person, but not too much like a politician at a lie detector.

Where are your arms? Straight down on your sides like a robot? Nope. Folded? Nope, that is a very closed signal. Hold them wherever you would hold them if you were talking to a guy friend. If you're sitting on a couch, if she gets closer to you, the back of the couch is fine.

Where are your feet? Pointed towards her, right? If not, you're not as interested as you thought.

Where are your eyes? They're on her eyes. They don't stray below the neck. You're not subtle. Bonus points if you get to the point, she takes her top off and you *still* look her in the eyes. If maintaining eye contact is hard, look at the bridge of her nose. Point out things in the room so you have an excuse to not make eye contact. Point out people in the room and make up stories about them.

Tone of voice. Do you always sound grumpy? Work on injecting a smile into your voice and eyes. This may mean watching Simpsons more, or whatever makes you giggle.

2.5 How to Never Run Out of Things to Say

Those questions I pulled out of my ass a few sub chapters ago- I've never heard them. I've never said them. I just make shit up. It's a gift! Try those. Then really *listen* to what she has to say. Remember it. Use it in conversation. I'm telling you, my shit is gold! I would totally get the ladies if I were a dude! I still get the ladies! Not as much as when I had a truck and a Labrador instead of a power wheelchair and a chihuahua, but either way, I probably get hit on by more chicks than whoever's reading this, and probably whoever wrote all the other ones. So listen up!

Seriously. Really *listen*. If she just responds to the "How are you?" with a "good, you?", you can make fun of the way "How are you?" doesn't mean anything anymore. It means "I acknowledge your presence." Ask her how she *really* is or ask her why she's good. If you actually listen, you can respond appropriately and never run out of things to say. I'm not even going to look up the men written chapters because I've already written half the words it asked for, and I'm only in chapter two. And I added four more chapters.

But this is the only book you'll ever need. I know what women want way more than a bunch of dudes do, no matter what they wrote their theses on (mine was on The Simpsons, BTW).

Chapter 3

How to Tell if a Woman is Interested in You

Okay, don't take it personally, but it might personally apply to you. Men are idiots. The depth of their stupidity continues to astound me! Let me replay a conversation I had in college with a friend.

Me: Guys are so dumb. You say hi to him, and he thinks you want him. You bring him a plate of cookies, and he thinks, "What a nice girl."

Him: We're not that dumb. .... Does Laura like me?

Me: Yeah, why?

Him: She brought me a plate of brownies yesterday, and I thought, "What a nice girl."

Dude, when we like you, we're not very subtle either! I suppose I do think more like a dude, as I miss it too often. But I think more like a woman, because I **am** one, than any dude writing this shit. But seriously, you guys are worse than I am. Let me replay another conversation my coworker replayed to me. She was a therapist, I was the receptionist. I've had a lot of jobs. She was doing group. All her clients were male.

One client: I got a new mail lady.

Every other client: Yeah, man!

First client: She said hi to me.

Other clients: Yeah, man!!!!

First client: Do you think she wants to have sex with me?

Other clients: Yeah!!! (Fist bumping, high fives ensue around the room)

Therapist: No! No! No! She was just being friendly! That's her job! She's not interested in you!

First client: Oh. Do you think she wants to have sex with me?

I really wish these two conversations were isolated events. But being a guys' girl, guys talk to me like I'm one of the guys. I'm privy to these conversations all the time. They're not isolated events.

Think about it. Pretty woman smiles at you, you think she wants to have sex with you. Not-so-attractive chick smiles at you, she's a creeper, amirite?

We do the same thing except we just assume **all** men want to have sex with us, and the ugly ones usually **are** creepers. So are the good-looking ones, but we let it slide. The Halo effect.

A smile is just a smile. It doesn't mean she's interested. What does?

- Following you around at a party
- Laughing at your jokes, especially if they're lame (which is usually)
- Playing with her hair or jewelry while talking to you
- Orienting her feet towards you. Pay attention to people's feet. Where their feet point is a subconscious indicator of where they want to be.
- Calling or texting you just to say hi

- Asking you to help her

- Offering to help you

3.1 Seven Common Indicators You May be Missing

I had to look this one up as well. Surprise, surprise, all the articles I found were written by dudes. Having said that, don't listen to the other articles. I will tell you where these are right, and where they're complete malarkey.

1. She mirrors you or your actions

   People do mirror each other subconsciously. They begin to walk in sync with their "work husbands" or friends they're interested in. We do it. You do it. But this one's so subconscious, most people don't notice it at all.

2. Proximity

   How close or far apart is she standing to you? Notice how close or far apart she is with other people, especially other men. Maybe she's just a close talker. She follows you at a party or is often in your work area. She scoots her desk closer to you. These signs are not very subtle. You're a dumbass if you miss them, but we still like you.

3. She lightly touches her erogenous zones—neck, thighs, wrists, hair, behind the ears.

   I'm calling bullshit on this one. Hair, jewelry, sure. But she's not touching herself all over. And if she is, she might have a medical condition, like fibromyalgia. Yeah, I have that too. I'm fun.

4. She adjusts her clothing and reveals herself.

I'm calling bullshit on this one too. We do that to get out of speeding tickets, to pass classes, to make other women jealous, and to check our own selves out. Damn, I love my own boobies! Other women's, not so much. Sorry dudes, not everything we do, we do for you. Feel free to break out into song again.

5. She doesn't talk about or even mention other men.

Again, with the bullshit. She might talk about other men because she's nervous. She might do it to make you jealous. She might do it to see how you'd react. She might do it because she doesn't know what to talk about either. Hell, I do it to guys I like because I'm awkward! You know what they say, if you can't do, teach. But I really can-do public speaking. But not being awkward in front of your crush? Inside all of us, the all the cool people anyway, lives a 12-year-old boy. We're all awkward. She also might talk *not* a problem about about other guys because she sincerely likes the *subject* you're talking about.

6. She points her feet your way.

That, yes. That's been proven by peer-reviewed academic journals in both nonverbal communications and psychology. If she catches you staring, just say cute shoes. The worst-case scenario is that she would think you're gay, you become BFF's, you wait until she says she wishes you were straight. Bam! She'll probably take it right back, but she might not.

7. She inquiries about the women in your life.

Also bullshit. She might just be nosy. I mean, she might be doing it out of interest, but it seems like a red flag to me. Like, "oh, who's Susan? You didn't tell me about her when we met. You must be cheating on me." In her defense, most men cheat. But this is good for me to read so I know what to so a guy knows I'm interested. I usually just straight tell him, but clearly that hasn't worked. I'll start taking notes on his female cousins, his former bosses, and his childhood friends.

3.2 How to Flirt Back with Her

I have no idea how to flirt with a woman. On purpose. I've apparently hit on many on accident. Clearly, I suck at flirting with men too. Actually, I don't. I just ghost if he's the normal douchebag type. But I looked up what women want from men- written by a man, of course, to see what I was missing. Because I'm called a flirt all the time, and I rarely do it on purpose. I suck at it when it's deliberate. So let me say this: if she's just friendly and outgoing, that doesn't mean she's flirting with you. If she's just kind and polite, that doesn't mean she's flirting with you.

The stuff the other articles said was bullshit. Don't listen to them. Here's how to flirt with a woman:

Step 1. Make eye contact.

Step 2. Smile.

Step 3. Approach her.

Step 4. Say "Hi. How are you?"

You saw that coming, didn't you? Then, just have a conversation. If you're sitting on a couch, put your arm on the back of it. Not around her. Don't touch her. If she sorts of snuggles into you, go ahead and rest your hand on her shoulder. If she doesn't, keep your arm on the couch. You're not touching her.

Just have a normal conversation. Treat her like a human being. Don't stare at her tits. Just appreciate her company. Throw some compliments that have nothing to do with looks in. I'll help you out.

"That's really interesting. How did you get into that field? / I wouldn't have seen it from that perspective if you hadn't just said that./ How did you learn that? You must be really smart."

The best part about that start is, you don't even to like the subject. Interesting is kind of a neutral word. But I'll give you some more.

"Wow, you really have an eye for detail. I wouldn't have noticed that. Do you notice all minutiae or just in things that interest you?"

Bonus points (from me) if a dude actually uses the word minutiae in a sentence.

"I totally agree with you on that point, but I was kind of hoping for a healthy debate because you seem really witty. So, I have to say something controversial to get that debate going. Coke and Pepsi are the same thing! Wake up, people!"

If you want to start a healthy debate but you agree with her, or you don't want to discuss religion or politics (good call), make a silly controversial point.

"Your outfit is so well put together. You must teach me how to match! And the difference between mauve and magenta!"

Again, it's silly. But it's a compliment she'll remember.

3.3 How to Talk about Yourself in an Attractive Way

Your tone of voice says more about you than your words. Do you have a crappy job because the economy sucks? Don't be embarrassed about it. Give it a better name if you want, but don't sound dejected when you tell her what you do. You sound like a loser with a lame job when you do that.

Make it sound more interesting. And if you can't, tell her what you're trying to get into while you work your lame job or how amazing the benefits are.

Tell her how great your kids are. If you talk about your ex, speak well of her. And again, self-deprecating humor never fails. Unless you're a female trying to make some female friends. Never mind. I don't need any more. Both of mine are awesome.

You might say something like, "My kid's probably a genius. Just saying. He probably got that from his mother."

This shows her that you don't talk shit on people. She feels safer knowing if she fucks it up with you, you're not going around saying horrible things. If that was too kind and you want to backtrack, say something like, "Only 16 years old and already knows the days of the week. God bless his mother's genes."

Now it's just funny, and of course, you'll have to say you're kidding. But leave it at that. Don't talk shit on your exes.

If you have a hard time talking about yourself, talk about where you grew up or places you've traveled.

But if you're a good listener, you don't *have* to talk about yourself. You just listen intently and ask probing, appropriate questions that show her you've been listening.

A good *listener,* is, by default, an excellent conversationalist. Because no one really remembers what you said. They just remember how you made them feel. And actually, *listening* to a woman, instead of trying to fix her problems, or playing on your phone or checking out other women, or waiting to talk, or just pretending to listen until you get laid, makes her feel pretty special.

The best way to talk about yourself in an attractive manner is to talk about your goals and your passions, no matter how "nerdy" they are.

Whatever makes your eyes light up when you're talking about it, that's adorable.

Remember when you were a kid and you wanted to be a fireman and a dolphin trainer and a race car driver and a king? That little kid is still inside you, and he comes out a little bit when you talk about your passion. Don't lose that.

3.4 Be Genuinely Interested in What She Has to Say

If what she's talking about bores you, like how many calories she ate that day, god, I was bored just writing that- anyway, if she bores you, try to bring the conversation around to something else.

"Calories only exist if you count them. You said you had a dog? What kind?"

Also, if she's talking about calories or what she ate or, god, I can't even finish writing this. Hang on. I need to go find something greasy and deep fried if I finish that sentence. Anyway, if she's talking about shit like that, she's fishing for a compliment. If you take the bait, you'll have to convince her she's not fat and she's beautiful a few times until you get bored and say, "Fine, you win. You're fat and ugly. Can we talk about your dog now?" At which point, she'll go off crying. Yeah, I see why I don't have a lot of female friends. The ones I do have are also no bullshitters. I suggest you don't even take the bait. Tell her she's gorgeous when she's not asking for it. It means more to both of you. PS. Fat is not synonymous with ugly. I'm pretty freaking sexy.

Any who, steer the conversation back to your common interests. If you don't have any, she's not the one for you.

If she's talking about her interests in a not so thinly veiled attempt to receive compliments, listen. Actually listen. Maybe it is cross stitch or law or drainage studies or teaching. If this is something that makes her happy, you need to know about it. You need to actually care. She's listening better than you think when you're talking about your hobbies.

Watch her eyes light up at different parts. Don't ever make fun of her dreams. She's still got that little kid inside her too. Being an adult means you know when it's appropriate to be a kid.

3.5 Once You Know She's Interested in You, How to Physically Escalate with Her

I probably should read what the men have to say on this subject just to be able to be more specific about their bullshit. But I won't. It's all bullshit. Listen to *me*. What're my qualifications? I'm a fucking woman! I'm not spending my life *trying* to fuck women! I don't think men realize how easy it is for a woman to get laid. The way they beg and offer amazing sex like their penis is magical. What's that song lyric by Garfunkel and Oates? I wouldn't touch your dick if I were poisoned and the antidote was in your sperm. Yeah. I've sent that song to a few guys. I mean, if their sperm could cure all *five* of my chronic illnesses, maybe. But I'm actually doing better on disability than I was working with a master's. Go 'Merica.

Okay, so we've determined she's interested in you and anything a man says on how to escalate it from here is complete bullshit, and women might send you that song. Okay, what's next?

Let her pick the pace for being physical. Go ahead and put your arm around her while you're watching a movie. Don't do the stretch, arm around the girl move. Just put your arm around her. That shows confidence. At this point, you know she likes you, right? If she backs away, she was being polite and she doesn't like you. Back away, not today.

There may come a time when it just *feels* right to kiss her. Still ask. Even if you've started to kiss her. Pull back and ask, "Is this okay?" Always get consent. Always, always, always. If she doesn't **say** yes or physically kiss you back, pull back, keep your arm around her, and say, "When you're ready." You don't have to apologize if you stopped, you hadn't felt her up, you'd just kissed her then backed away, not today.

Respecting her space and going at her pace is a **huge** turn on.

Let her put her arm on your leg. At this point, go ahead and "subtly" check her out. You think you're being subtle, but we know. We always know. The Point of View Gun won't work on us; we're already women. But at this point, she *wants* you to check her out. She might even "subtly" give you a better show. She knows she's not being subtle, but you think she thinks she is. It's cute.

Go ahead and play with her hair if she leans into you. PS. We *love* that. Yes, I'm speaking for all women on that one.

When you leave at the end of the night, and all you've done is cuddle, she's *really* into you. We love cuddling. Go ahead and kiss her forehead or the top of her head.

She might make the first move towards the actual kiss that begins something real (you're not being a dick and leading her on just to get laid, are you? Don't do that. She's a real person.), or she might be waiting for you to make the first move.

Chapter 4

End Game

The endgame is marriage, living together, or an exclusive long-term relationship. This is another area where you're probably moving at different paces.

She might want to move this one along faster than you want. Let her know you're not ready for that. But under no circumstances should you promise to marry her if you have no intention of doing so.

Maybe you need to live together first. Maybe your religion prohibits sex before marriage, and you follow it.

However, the end game is going to work between you two, you need to communicate about it.

4.1 How not to Get Her to Leave with You

Let's backtrack a little bit. Okay. We're at the bar. We *haven't* had the sex I described earlier (I know my memory's bad, but I think I'd remember *that*). You've chatted with her. You've given some memorable openers (you're welcome, by the way), and now you want her to leave with you.

I'm gonna be totally honest because that's who I am. I've only ever seen that in the movies. When I go out to a bar or club or whatever, I'm usually with a group of friends. We came together, we leave together. To quote my father, "Go home with the one who brung ya." He's actually educated; it's just an old expression.

I've never seen any of my friends leave with a guy, even if they've been chatting with him all night. That's not terribly likely either. We go out to have fun with our friends. We really *don't* go out to get laid.

Until you ask a woman for help on how to talk to women, you'll just keep repeating the same bullshit that isn't working and not know *why* it's not working. Lucky I am writing up this piece. And added a few more chapters. Why women do the shit we do is *really* what you want to know.

So here it is on how to get her to leave with you: don't. Don't expect it. She came out to have fun with her friends. The best you can do is get her number. Let's talk about that now.

4.2 How to Get Her Number

You came out with your friends, she came out with hers, you all just came out to have a good time.

If you're chatting her up, be sure to introduce your friends. She'll introduce hers. Get a friendly competition going on. What kind of bar is it? Karaoke? Pub trivia? Sports? Whatever it is, you can get a friendly competition among your friends. You can invent one. Start asking random trivia to each other, no phones allowed.

You're having fun with your friends, she's having fun with her friends, this is why you came out. Now it's a little awkward to buy her a drink, so don't. Just keep chatting with both groups.

Say, "Hey, you're pretty cool. Mind if I call you sometime? I had a lot of fun tonight." Chances are, you'll get a few numbers, even if it's obvious you were only interested in her. Take all their numbers, add them all on Facebook, but only try to date her. We talk, remember?

Don't play games like "I lost my phone; will you call it?" What are you, 12? Just grow some ovaries and ask her for her number. Why do I say ovaries instead of balls? Because women get shit done, and your balls don't seem to be doing much good if you're playing stupid games.

Don't, under **any** circumstances, wait three days to call her. That's stupid bullshit that doesn't work in real life. Does it even work in the movies?

If you've been chatting with her friends and your friends all night, chances are, she's giving you a real number. Still, don't call it right then.

Give her a goodnight text a few hours after you get home. Like, "Hey, I had fun tonight. Have a good night." If she doesn't text back, call it. If it's a fake number, sorry, bro.

Don't allude to sex, don't call her pet names like sweetie, sweetheart, honey, babe..... any of that shit. When we don't know you, it feels like you're being possessive of us, like we're property. We're not property. We're human beings. Just because you find us beautiful doesn't mean you own us.

4.3 How to Go from Getting Her Phone Number to the First Date

Okay, so you've gotten her number, and it's not a fake (time and temperature was my go-to fake number, but the rejection hotline is pretty funny). How to get a date?

Don't ask it in a text. Don't ask to "meet up" or "hang out" or "come over" or any of that. Call her up and say these words: "Would you like to go on a date with me?"

You guys had a good time at the bar, you met her friends, she met yours. Everything's peachy. She either says yes or makes up some lame ass excuse or suddenly has a boyfriend. Back away, not today. Much of this was covered in Chapter 1.1 under Confidence.

Plan it. Don't make her plan it. She's sick of that shit. She's not your mommy, she didn't carry you in her womb for nine months. Feel free to break out into song again.

Okay, she's said yes, you have a specific date in mind. Plan it. Go to a dueling piano bar or The Rocky Horror Picture Show or whatever it is you've planned. In this scenario, you've already met in person. Offer to pick her up. She'll probably allow it since she's met you in real life now.

Bring flowers or maybe just a single one for the first date. You want to make a good impression. Does she have a black thumb and kill any plant that comes near her? Maybe bring those edible flowers or an origami one. Not chocolates just yet. Do something that makes you stand out. Asking on a real, actual date and bringing flowers would stand out. I'm pretty sure that's happened never to me. I've been asked out on a few real, actual dates, and I've been given flowers, but not simultaneously.

4.4 What to Talk About on the First Date

You should've done your homework by now. Either you met online, where she has a profile you've read by now, and you've been chatting for a few days or weeks, or you met in real life, most likely through work or mutual friends, or at the bar scene with everybody's friends. If you met in real life, you've probably hung out a few times with the gang, and you've definitely chatted and texted.

Don't go into the first date blind, unless it's a blind date, in which case you have to, and your friends probably suck at setting people up anyway. "You're both single! You have so much in common!" Next.

"You teach college. You could help him get his GED and get back on track!" What's in it for me? I actually *enjoy* my own company too much to spend my time with losers.

Okay, so you've done your homework. You know her interests, a few of them, anyway. You have at least a few common interests. Again, if not, it's not gonna work out. Just saying.

Start with the stuff you've already been talking about. If you haven't been talking to/ texting/ communicating in some manner with her for at least a week, it's too soon for a first date.

Send her good morning at good night texts. Not only does that subconsciously tell her that she's the last thing you think about before you go to bed and the first thing you think about when you wake up in the morning, but you're also subconsciously ensuring she does the same for you.

I get dating a few people at a time to see what you want. A lot of women do that. *I* do that. But if she's the one the really want to be with, don't do that. She might be doing that. That's fine. Let her. Follow my two cardinal rules, and you'll soon discover the rest of the competition is melting away. If I ever meet someone I really want to be with, who either asks me out or says yes, I'll date only him. Until then, yeah, still sifting.

But you had someone in mind when you clicked on this, didn't you? You're picturing her now, aren't you? You're probably thinking you'll never get to a first date with her.

You might and you might not. The worst that can happen is that you follow my two cardinal rules and become a better man and develop more confidence and meet someone else later.

It's never too late. I legit live in a retirement home because of all my fun autoimmune diseases. Finally, I'm on the young side somewhere! And my fourth-grade teacher was wrong! She said our generation wouldn't get social security! I beat the system. You're all screwed. But I see or hear about couples getting together often. Some, it's just a fuck, and everybody knows it and nobody cares because we're all adults, except their kids, who've forgotten that. They're old, they're not dead! Some, it's actual marriage, and not all of them have been married before. I don't know if waiting until you're 70 gives you hope or despair, but there it is.

But you know her interests *before* the date. You've talked a few times. Talk about those. My particular geographical society has a lot of people waiting for marriage before they have sex, so there are a lot of 20-year-old newlyweds. This is why I'm old. There are also a lot of 24-year-old divorcees around here. A friend of mine had a test whenever her college friends were engaged. The three things you *must* know about a man before you marry him: his middle name, his cell phone provider, and his favorite Disney movie. She uses these because they're things that should come up in normal conversation before you get married. Don't force the issue. If you randomly tell her your middle name or your cell phone provider, that's weird.

But if you tell her what or who you were named after, your middle name will come up. Then she'll tell you about her name.

And *everyone* has a favorite Disney movie, even if you haven't seen it since you were a kid. On that note, Toy Story 3 was a real tear jerker and made me hate Emily (who happens to be Andy's mom) for leaving her toys, until a different friend said, "Fuck you for growing up, Emily!" Now it's kinda manipulative. We all grow up to some extent. Or should.

And here are a few things that you *should* talk about at some point before commitment: hopes, dreams, fears, shattered dreams (don't try to fix them for her; you've got a few of your own too), unrealistic dreams (don't tell her they're realistic; you've got a few of your own too, I hope), real fears, not like clowns or spiders, but emotional fears, like losing loved ones, never feeling loved, commitment (some of us are afraid of that too. I'm terrified), fear of failure, fear of success, what she hopes people will say at her funeral, that type of stuff. Although I wouldn't suggest talking about funerals on a first date. But my parents met at one, and they're coming up on their 52nd anniversary, so what do I know? Those things are probably too intense for a first date, but in time, you should know those things about each other.

4.5 How to Get Her to Go Home with You

Let her pick the pace for the physical stuff. You'll get there. Keep asking her on real, actual dates. Let her ask you on real, actual dates. Whoever asks pays and plans. Let her pay for it if she asked you.

When I waitressed and people would fight over who got the check, I *always* gave it to the woman. My coworkers would usually just put it in the middle and run away or give it to the man. But this is another reason I got better tips than they did. When the man would angrily ask (which happened *every* time) why I gave it to her, I'd say that women scared me more. Everyone laughed because women are terrifying (and they *do* scare me more), and she'd leave a good tip and he'd slip some cash under the plate and she'd pretend she didn't see it. You're not subtle. We always see your shit, even if we don't call you on it.

Don't expect sex on the third date. That's not some magical number that has some legally binding contract. To her, it's probably still just a date.

You can trick a woman into sleeping with you, you can even trick a woman into loving you. But if you do either, you're exactly like every other douchebag out there.

She'll come home with you when she's ready. You probably need to have the DTR before she'll be ready. My brother-in-law thought that meant Dump The Retard. Sometimes it does. If you don't know, it means Define The Relationship.

Are you exclusive before you have sex? If you're long-term minded, the answer should be yes. Are you planning to get married, or just live together?

She'll come home with you when she's ready. Don't push her.

4.6 How to Handle Resistance to Sex

Seriously, just back off. Whining, begging, pleading, forcing—that's annoying and/or illegal. Treat us like we're human beings. "But what about my boner?" Jack off, dumbass. Not my problem. We prefer foreplay to actual sex.

Studies have actually been done to determine when a woman has more orgasms, being eaten out or sex. Actual penetration doesn't actually hit our sweet spot. My life made so much more sense after I read that. And it's about damn time studies are being done about women's orgasms. We totally get shit on, but the multiple orgasms *almost* makes up for it. Oh, by the way, we have more when you go down on us. As a woman, I can tell you that's true.

Do we fake them? All the damn time. But be more concerned about what *she* wants, and you'll get what you want. That's how most women work. There are the high maintenance, usually vapid ones. Save them for the meathead jocks. Oh, god, they're reproducing? <shudder> But average joes don't tend to like high maintenance chicks. Again, beauty fades. Crazy is forever. Choose your battles wisely.

And back the fuck off when we say no. I get it. I get how you've been trained since birth by every damn movie out there. The good guy "deserves" to get the girl. And she must be a 10. And *of course,* you're a good guy. So what gives? Why can you only seem to land fat chicks who are pretty, but not 10's? Because this isn't a fucking movie, even if America feels like a Jerry Springer show. But I get it. She's just "playing hard to get." She actually wants you. So no means maybe, and maybe means yes, so no means yes, right? Wrong! NO MEANS NO!!!!!!

So back off. Don't call her names. Back off at *any* point she says stop. You could be almost there, and she says, I don't want to do this. You could be not even close and she says, stop, you're hurting me. You could be almost at the point of insertion and she says, I changed my mind about losing it to you. Which brings up another point: if it comes up in conversation that she's a virgin, **do not say**, "challenge accepted." She wasn't offering you a challenge. Now she doesn't even want to hang out with you.

Stop when she says stop. Go home and jack off. Treat her like a human being and back off when she says to. The two cardinal rules that will turn even the most socially retarded, which is far beyond awkward, among you, into a ladies' man. Okay, it won't. But it'll probably turn you into a lady's man in the singular, which is the end game, right?

Chapter 5

Keeping Her Attracted to You,
or How to Have a Long-Term Relationship

Clearly, no man has done it for me yet. Except for Darrin. I liked him from kindergarten all the way until the fifth grade when I decided he was immature. That's the longest I've ever liked someone. My longest relationship though was with my Labrador. Seventeen years. May she Rest In Peace.

But if any man I'd liked had followed my two cardinal rules, things would be different. But apparently, I only go for douchebags. More on that later.

But treat her like a human being, and back off when she says to. This means ALWAYS. But let's see what the men have to say, and why it's probably manipulative bullshit.

Alright, I actually agree with every single heading I found on the first list I googled. I'll give you the heading, then my own take- a woman's perspective.

1. Act respectfully when you are with her.

    First, I'll change the title. *Be* respectful *at all times*. This goes back to the kindness bit. Don't talk shit about her to your friends. If you both keep your fights and arguments between just the two of you, your friends and family won't have a skewed opinion of the person you love most. Because we always seem to forget to tell them when our SO apologized.

It says to open doors, pull out chairs, give her your jacket when she's cold, all that stuff. I'll add to that. If she opens the door for you, just walk through it. If she wants to pay, just say thank you.

It says to pick your clothes more carefully and have proper hygiene. Hell to the yes!

Avoid any offensive actions in public, like swearing or belching. Okay, I'm obviously not the one to tell you not to swear. Or belching, for that matter. But do edit yourself in public on both accounts. And do I really need to add farting? I mean, I get that it happens, but try to make it the silent but deadly type and blame it on the dog. Although she'll know after a while. And if you have to rip a loud one in public, at least make it funny. Once, when I was subbing, I dropped a silent one as I walked past the popular kid. I was like, "Duuude!" I don't know if he was still popular the next day. I was just the sub. Not my problem.

Carry her books and backpack for her between classes or after school. Okay, I'll call bullshit on this one. If you're in high school or college, you have your own shit to carry. If you're an adult not in college, it's moot. But the whole damsel in distress bullshit is sexist. Like we can't take care of ourselves. Yeah, a lot of women play up that stereotype. If you'll remember, guys leave me watching a movie on my own because I don't "need" them. Well, not so much anymore. Now that I'm a wheelchair, I apparently always "need" them. I really don't. It's hard, but I'm learning to ask for and accept help with doors and shit. From men or women. Or children. Don't carry her shit or give her your hoodie (which you're never getting back, by the way. I have a collection of hoodies I didn't pay for) until she asks you to. If she looks like she's struggling, offer to help. If she looks cold

58

or says she is, offer your hoodie. Don't just rush in. Offer first.

2. Compliment her and be genuine about it.

    Don't take the bait when she's fishing. Instead, call her out. Say something like, "I know you're fishing and I don't want to take the bait. Wouldn't you rather my compliments be sincere?" Then make sure you sincerely compliment her. They don't all have to be about her looks, either. I gave you a bunch of compliments to choose from earlier, but here are a few more. Be sure to compliment her on the things she's most self-conscious about. If it is about looks, be specific. Like, "I love your crooked nose. Seriously. It adds character." "I think the gap in your teeth is adorable! I really do." "You really don't need bigger boobs. They're perfect for me. Besides, you don't want the back problems those other girls have" (she really doesn't). But let's give a few examples not about looks. Because you're thinking of her now, aren't you? You're thinking of the tiny little details about her that you know/ think/ fear she hates- her freckles, her weight, her hair, her height- you're thinking of it because you *do* find it adorable, amirite? Tell her that. Moving right along.

    - I love your laugh. It's adorable. It makes me smile.

    - I love the way your eyes light up when you talk about...

    - I love the feeling I have when I see you like everything's gonna be okay.

    - I love the teamwork we have when we do this...

    - I love coming home to you.

- I love waking up to you.

- I love your smell.

- I love you even more than your dog.

<Okay, don't out and out lie. That's not even possible.>

- You're really good at…

- You're really smart at…

3. Let Her Know She is on Your Mind

You don't need to text her all day, and you don't even need to respond immediately. If she's an actual adult, she'll get that you're busy. She is too. But text her at least once a day with more than, "Sup?" Ask a specific question about her day, or send an inside joke, or just say, "Hey, just thinking about you. Hope you have a good day." We find that cute, and if it's not all day long, you're a fully functional adult with a job and a life. But if it's at least a little bit, we're still an important part of that life.

4. Surprise Her with Romantic Gestures

Yes. Do this. The article I read suggested a playlist of songs that remind you of her. Yes. Do that. If you have an "our song," it needs to be first. Do not include Stupid Girl or You're a Bitch or any rap song about stupid ass hoes. You're welcome.

The article also suggested slipping love notes into her locker. Okay, we're talking about the long haul here, people. The M word. Or at the very least, the F word. No, not the Fuck word. We can get that anywhere. The Future word. Yeah, high schoolers know who they want to marry, but they have no idea how to do their taxes. Or that they'll need to.

The love notes is a good idea, but if you're in high school, focus on your studies, kid. Just throw a few in her car's console someday. Put some in your hoodie pocket. The hoodie you know she's going to borrow and never return.

Ask to borrow her car someday. Return in fully washed, with a full tank of gas, and a dozen roses on the seat. She'll rave about that for months.

Do these as preventive measures instead of fixes. It's a lot easier that way.

The list suggests to get her something she can wear every day to remind her how much you care. Okay, no. Was this written by a man? Men don't know how to shop for women's clothes. They barely know how to shop for their own. We're perfectly capable of choosing our own wardrobe, thanks.

I'll give a few suggestions of real ones. The love notes and playlists are good. My car wash idea is good. Here's a few more.

- Notice what's in her fridge. Bring her groceries based on her tastes occasionally.

- Send her a book about her celebrity crush.

- Randomly put money in her PayPal.

- Buy her surprise gifts from Amazon. Everyone likes surprise presents! Stuff she'd like, maybe body spray and lotion gift baskets, movies she hasn't gotten around to buying, pictures similar to the ones hanging in her house already.

- Plan a picnic someplace unusual- the mountains, a rooftop, the bed of a truck.

5. Have Fun & Make Her Laugh

Yeah, everybody likes to laugh. Include plenty of banter in your relationship. Don't get all butthurt if you walk into one and she picks it up. Be disappointed in her if you accidentally lay 'em down and she doesn't pick 'em up. If she walks into one, ya gotta take it. Them's the rules.

But make sure you don't tickle her if she doesn't like it. Make sure you're not making fun of her for something that actually hurts. When she tells you to back off, do.

The two cardinal rules: treat her like she's human and back off when she says to- they're not just about sex. They're for all the time. If she says she doesn't want to talk about it, try believing her instead of forcing her to talk when she's still upset and her words won't come out right. Just back off.

5.1 The Beginning of the End or the End of the Beginning

This was originally supposed to be the last chapter, but I added Consent because no one seems to know what that is, and Why Women Do the Crazy Things They Do. You're welcome.

This is supposed to be the happily ever after chapter, right? You liked it so you put a ring on it, game over. I realize Beyoncé *is* a woman, so I don't know why she refers to us as "it." Ouch.

But my jaded brain just came up with a new expression. Seriously, as I wrote "happily ever after." How's about "trappily ever after"? I'm good, I know.

Because if your endgame was to get her to say yes, as long as she actually loved you, all you had to was ask.

Now that she's good and duped, you're free to cheat, right? No? Then why do so many men do it?

Keep her loving you. Not because you don't want her to cheat, although you don't, but because **you still love her.** And on that note, it's not the spouse's job to keep either one from cheating, and it's not their fault if they do. If you're big enough to get married or live together, you're big enough to keep your pants on your own damn self.

Keep doing the love notes, the surprise gifts, the date nights, even-especially-if you have kids. Keep the love notes you gave each other. Go through them after a big fight to remind yourselves who you were when you got married, before life got in the way. And if you keep doing them, then it's not the same ten notes after every fight. That'll only work for two, maybe three fights.

Ignore a lot of that well-meaning but useless or actually bad marriage advice you heard.

Like "never go to bed angry." That's bullshit. You can go to bed angry. Don't make a habit of it, of course. But what's more likely if you try to follow that- a: you resolve your issues and it's not the same fight you have all the time, or b: it is the same fight, you stay up, getting more tired and more angry, saying things you'll regret in the morning, but by the time morning comes, you're too pissed at what they said to apologize for what you said? That's what I thought. Go to bed angry. It's okay. Just go to bed. You'll see it more clearly in the morning.

Or "marriage is 50/50." Marriage isn't 50/50. An ideal marriage is

100/100. You're each giving 100% of what you have. That's going to vary on the person, on the day. I have five chronic illnesses. I can't do what other people can do. If I had a husband, he'd need to be an amazing caliber of man who would recognize that, and not just think that I'm lazy.

Why is a single person giving marriage advice? Because I don't have a failed marriage under my belt, or several. I don't have a "successful" marriage that spans a few decades, but we've grown so complacent we either don't talk anymore or we just fight, and we're too old and scared to actually address our problems or start over. I've seen a lot of marriages. I've seen a lot fail, and I've seen a lot fail but look like they succeed. I've seen a few succeed.

Be one of those few. Marry her if you say you're going to. If living together was the agreement at the onset and marriage wasn't on the table, and she changes her mind a few years down the road, that's a discussion that needs to be revisited until you have a compromise, you're both happy with. If that compromise included giving her a date, follow through. Not all women *need* marriage. Some are happy living together.

Marriage, or commitment, shouldn't be the end of your freedom, the end of your male friends. Male friendships are even *more* important after you've "settled down." We make sure women still have female friendships, so what gives? Another shitty double standard, this time where you guys get the short end of the stick. But they all suck.

It *is* the end of an era. But it doesn't have to be the beginning of a depressing new era. If you've found the right person, you didn't lose your freedom. You found a permanent plus one who will be bored with you at boring events, or play tic tac toe, and a permanent friend.

Don't play into that "men don't express their emotions" bullshit. If you can talk to her when you're irritated, you don't have to wait until you're angry and then have a screaming match.

Like Semisonic says, "Every new beginning comes from some other beginning's end."

Chapter 6

Consent

No one really understands consent. We're taught to go along to get along, don't make waves, don't rock the boat. You're taught that boys will be boys, and she didn't "say" no.

But she didn't say yes, either. Humans have more than fight or flight. We have fight, flight, or freeze. And most victims freeze. If she says stop, and you don't, she'll probably freeze. Because she said it. You ignored her. Now you're going to do whatever the hell you want, and she can't stop you.

What if her body put her in fight mode? Even if she's bigger than you, you're still probably stronger than her. You don't know why she's fighting, so you fight back to restrain her because she suddenly went crazy on you.

What if her body had gone into flight mode? Where's she gonna go? Especially if you're already on top of her.

Listen when she says stop. Or ow. Or I don't want to. Or nothing at all but her body language clearly indicates she's nervous or scared. One out of four women has been a victim. It might not be about you. But it might. What are you doing? If she's tense, don't offer a massage. Back off and ask what would help her relax.

Here's a poem in a book I found on Amazon called Don't Call it a Fu**ing Journey (Abridged).

What Changed?

He's four and pushes her in the mud.

The adults say you must like her.

He's twelve and snaps her bra strap.

The adults say you're just playing.

He's fifteen and wrestles her too roughly.

The adults say you really like her.

He's eighteen and pulls her hair.

Now it's abuse.

What changed?

She's four and says I don't like that.

The adults say he must like you.

She's twelve and says I don't like that.

The adults say he's just playing.

He's fifteen and wrestles her too roughly.

The adults say he really likes you.

She's eighteen and says I don't like that.
People say you should've said something sooner.

What changed?

He's four and pushes other kids.

Mommy didn't teach him well.

He's twelve and starts liking girls.

They shouldn't be so distracting.

He's fifteen and starts getting rejected.

She's just playing hard to get.

He's eighteen and keeps pressuring her.

Now it's rape.

What changed?

She's four and can't find clothing that covers.

Little girls shouldn't dress like that.

She's seven and the pants say "juicy."

Little girls aren't juicy!

She's twelve and wearing bras now.

Bras distract the boys!

She's fifteen and still can't find clothing that covers.

Little slut.

She's eighteen and said no.
Did you see what she was wearing?

She was asking for it.

I guess nothing changed.

Chapter 7

Why Women Do the Things They Do
(You're Welcome)

We do some crazy shit, not gonna lie. So do you guys, but here's the difference: you guys are pretty one-track-minded, and when you're with us, you're usually thinking about sex, so we think that's all you think about. When we're not around, you're thinking about work, or your car, or whatever else. But one at a time.

We're thinking about all that shit all at once. Yes, we do think about sex. With you. But that's not the only thing we're thinking about when we're together. That's usually the kind of thing we think about when we're apart. When we're together, we're thinking about all the shit in our lives, but we're also thinking about the cute stuff you said yesterday. Say more of that cute stuff. Do more of that cute stuff. If you're only thinking about sex when you're with us, we feel like objects. Again.

No matter how hot she is, somebody's tired of fucking her. Unless you view us as actual human beings. Unless you've trained your brain to think about more than one thing at a time. I'm not asking you guys to have an eight-lane highway like we have. But maybe upgrade from the one-lane dirt road, huh?

7.1 Why Women Ghost

You ghost. We ghost. Everybody ghosts. You guys ghost because you're no longer interested and you don't want that discussion. And that's fine. You don't owe us anything.

We ghost for the same reason and more. We also ghost because we've had men legit go violent on us for rejecting them. We ghost because we never *were* interested, and we're scared to say that. We ghost because we've been called horrible names for rejecting someone. You probably have been too, a time or two. With us, it seems like more often than not. We ghost because women legit get killed for rejecting a dude.

We ghost because it's easier and safer. When we ghost, just let us go. I mean, sure, text enough to know *that* we've ghosted, and we're not just legit busy. You can even ask if we've ghosted. If the answer is yes, you won't hear from us.

Again, the two cardinal rules: treat us like human beings and back off when we say to (or ghost). If she's ghosting on you, she's not the one for you.

Again, beauty fades but crazy is forever. Choose your battles wisely.

7.2: Why Women Lead You On

We don't do it on purpose, most of us. We really just are trying to be polite so we keep saying yes. Or we're scared to say no, so we keep saying yes. Or we keep "giving you another chance," even though we know we don't actually like you; we're hoping we will. Or we keep "giving you another chance" because you keep begging us to.

Sometimes we lead you on because we legit want a friend and dangling sex is the only way to keep most guys around. Because the actual "nice guy," who doesn't think he "deserves" sex for being a decent fucking human being, is really rare.

And then there are the women who constantly "need" a man- to fix shit, to be her buffer at weddings (okay, that's valid), to get her through yet another emotional crisis- the kind of women men ditch me for all the time because I don't "need" them. You guys need to be

71

needed. We exploit that. But if we actually sleep with you, you'll stop doing shit for us.

I can kill my own spiders. I cry to my female friends. But I still actually do need men sometimes. Or did, before I lived in a retirement home. Now if I have an issue, I just call maintenance, who are men, but it's their actual paid job. They don't expect sex.

So even the most independent women need men sometimes. Listen up, fellas! If you do that stuff without expecting to get laid, thinking you "deserve" sex, or even hoping, you become, get this- an actual nice guy. Long-term material. Until then, we have to dangle sex to keep you around. Once you get it, or once you for real realize it ain't gonna happen (even though we've told you a few times before), we never see you again.

So, often, we lead you on just to keep you around. We enjoy your *company*, but we have dangle sex to get even that. If we don't enjoy your company and we're still leading you on, we like the attention, or we're lonely, or we're bored. They're all dick moves, and I've been guilty of a few myself.

But mostly, we don't want to hurt you. Yes, we may be scared or manipulated into saying yes again. We may be hoping that if we spend enough time with you, we'll find you physically attractive, because you are, legit, an actual nice guy, who's not whining about being a nice guy (spoiler- those ones *aren't*). But really, we don't want to hurt you.

That's chickenshit, I know. We hurt you more by leading you on than ghosting. I know. We all know this. But that's future us' problem. Present us just doesn't want to hurt you.

Maybe that's something you can talk about on the first date. Might be awkward, but when wouldn't it be? It's easier if you grow some ovaries first and be totally honest about your feelings. Like, "Hey, I really like you and I'd like to see where this goes. If you don't feel the same about me, please just tell me instead of lead me on or ghost. I promise I won't go crazy or beg. I'll leave you alone. It'll just hurt less if you straight up tell me."

Actually, that's genius. If she didn't really know how she felt about you before the date, she likes you now. You've just shown her that you have feelings, that you're honest, and that you'll respect her boundaries. That's fucken gold, man! Again, you're welcome. My brain surprises even me sometimes.

7.3 Why Women Think the Way They Think

Again, we've got an 8-lane freeway. You've got a dusty dirt road. Even when you guys have ADD. You've just got a few dirt roads you jump on and off, and no one can keep up with you.

When *we* have ADD? Yes, women can have it too. And autism. I've only got ADD of those, though. I know, you're totally surprised. In my defense, these how-to pick-up women guides were all written by men. I don't feel like they go in totally chronological order, but I only read a few in order to write this book. And the how pick up men guides are probably all written by women. I've never actually read any of those. I don't feel like starting now; I'm no good when I actually *try*. Imagine if I *tried* to try. That sound catastrophic. And like a double negative. So, before I go off on my ADD tangent (I'm pretty proud of myself how much I've focused for this, actually), I'll start telling you why we think the way we think, because you probably skipped everything else and jumped to this chapter. Go back and read the rest. It's better than any other bullshit written by a man you've read. It's better than ten Superbowls.

Okay, we think the way we think due to the highly controversial and still hotly debated topic of nature vs. nurture.

The poem from earlier illustrates how boys and girls, who become men and women, are treated differently and given different expectations.

It's not that women are inherently bad at math and science. It's that they were *told* they were when they girls. It's that they "couldn't get their pretty little dresses dirty" when they tried.

It's not that men are inherently bad at cooking or childcare. It's that they were *told* they didn't need to know those skills. And when they were boys, they probably didn't. Neither did girls, probably. Boys were also told they were sissies for doing them. Then they grow up, and they *need* those skills if they're to survive in the adult world, and now they're sissies for *not* knowing them.

Let's be real, here. When it comes to nature, society has fucked us all over pretty well. And the non-binary people? They're totally fucked. But because I'm *not* non-binary, and I *am* female, I'm only going to discuss why women think the way they do as a whole. Obviously, if you want to know why "she" thinks the way she does- again, the one woman you clicked on this link in the first place for- you'll have to talk to her specifically. I'm only gonna help you out in the general sense.

In short, we've been conditioned. We've been conditioned into extremes.

Our voices have been silenced so often, we tend to either stop talking or start screaming. We wish people had listened to us when we just spoke.

Everything is our fault. So, we've been conditioned into accepting blame for everything, which *really* doesn't help our anxiety, or not accepting responsibility at all.

When a woman accuses a man of rape or sexual assault, the first question is *always,* "What was she wearing?" Why isn't the first question, "WHAT THE HELL IS HE DOING FUCKING RAPING PEOPLE?????"

I used to work at a treatment center for sex offenders (I told you, I've had a lot of jobs). Out of sheer curiosity once, over the course of a few weeks, I asked all my clients what their victim was wearing the first time. Not one of them remembered. Not one.

We have to change our routes home, park in well-lit areas, watch our drinks, wear the right thing, say and do the right thing, wear our hair the right way (no ponytails; they're easier for men to grab), or we run the risk of getting raped. But we run it anyway just by existing, and it's *still* somehow our fault.

So, we act paranoid. We don't want to meet you at your house or ours for a first date if we've met online. But if you're going to rape us, you're going to rape us, and it's gonna be the first date or the 700th. But we *have* to think about this shit all the time.

"Well you got drunk at a frat party, what did you expect?" A hangover. A fucking hangover. That's what we expected.

If you're going to cheat on us, you're going to cheat on us, no matter how amazing we are. But it's still somehow our fault. But if women cheat on men, it's totally her fault. She knew what she was doing.

We're always the evil seductress, and men can't help it. I'm calling bullshit on that one too. My father, grandfathers, uncles, cousins, nephews- everyone I'm related to- would never touch a woman without her explicit consent.

We have to work twice as hard for half as much. We have to constantly prove our ability, and disprove that we got to where we got by sex. Add women of color, or lesbians, or transgender women, and they have to work four times as hard for a quarter as much.

Disabled women, too. We just don't have the energy. Well, I don't.

And the worst part is, women are harder on us than men.

So, we have to analyze every option, probably a few times, in order to be heard without sounding like a bitch, to lead without being bossy, to put out fires we didn't start, and to mitigate the damage to our own skin from the fires other people tried to burn us with.

Be patient with us. We've had a hard couple of centuries.

7.4 Why Women Seem to Constantly Send Mixed Signals

Read the why we lead you on and we ghost your subchapters again. Or at all, if you skipped to this section.

We want to keep you around. We enjoy your company. We don't always want to have sex with you. Sometimes we'll take one for the team and sleep with someone we don't like. Sometimes we'll do it because we're afraid to say no.

Often, we've said "not yet" quite a few times and been ignored because you were horny. Down, boy. So we lie back and think of London to shut you up. We're more interested in the cuddling and the conversation.

And we fake orgasms because we have to. Yes, all of us. Every single one of us. Not every time, but every woman who's ever had sex with a man has faked an orgasm or two. It makes you do your job better. On that note, don't push on our heads when we're being kind enough to do the job we all hate. That's why it's called a job. We *hate* when you push on our heads. Yes, I've had a council with all women. Don't. Not ever. Just learn to fake it like we do.

If you listen to us the first time, we don't actually send as many mixed signals as you think. Back to the two cardinal rules: treat us like human beings, and back off when we say no.

If you offer a massage and we say no, don't try again with a foot massage or a hand massage or whatever. Sometimes we don't like to be touched. Sometimes we're just not in the mood.

If you ask what's wrong and we say "nothing," it means one of two things: actually, nothing *is* wrong, this is just my face, or I *really, truly* don't want to talk about it, and if you push me into an answer before I'm ready, the words won't come out right.

I get it. You've been conditioned to never take what a woman says at face value. And we've been conditioned to downplay our emotions all the time. Again, society has fucked us all up pretty well.

But try taking what she says at face value. If she gets upset that you didn't understand, *tell* her that you didn't understand.

I get it. I really do. My mom would point out that there was a rest stop coming up and get mad when my dad would drive right past. Yep, there sure was. He had no idea she was even *asking* him to stop (because she *wasn't*) until his five daughters made fun of their mother for it (behind her back) after they'd been married 40 years. Okay, most men don't have the advantage of five daughters, and very few of them could stay with a woman for 40 years.

But try this: next time she hints, and you don't get it because you won't, tell her she needs to outright ask. Not whine, manipulate, or beg. Try telling her straight that you're a man and by default, don't get hints.

When she hints for gifts, she feels like they mean less if she has to *ask* specifically for them. Pay attention to her likes and dislikes. Notice if she wears jewelry and what type.

Women aren't always the best at this either. I had one client when I worked at the daycare (I've had *a lot* of jobs) give me some beautiful earrings. I graciously said thank you and gave them to my sister rather than tell her my ears were no longer pierced.

While I'm on the subject, imma help you out a bit on gifts. Don't buy her clothes. You don't know how it's going to fit or look on her. She may carry her weight well or poorly. Other women suck at guessing my size and style, even women who see me often. I wouldn't even trust any of my gay guys to try. Don't give her cash (what are you, her uncle?), unless you do it creatively like in origami or in the shape of a cake.

Do pay attention to her books (if she doesn't read, I'm sad for you both. If you don't read, I'm sad for you both). Pay attention to her movie collection, the type of decor she has on the walls, and get something similar. Best way to do that: again, listen up, fellas! This shit is golden! Snap a pic of her with one of her pieces of art behind her. Take your phone into Home Goods or probably even Target in the home section, and ask a female employee what would go with this piece of art. Done and done! You've given her a gift she likes, without her having to ask or hint, and now you have a cute picture of her on your phone. Surely, she's got more than one piece of decor on her walls. Rinse and repeat. Take a picture of her bedspread and ask the employee what would match that. Are you guys taking notes? I really should teach a class on what women want. They're all taught by men, and they all suck.

Okay, I totally went off on a tangent there, but it was helpful. Anywho, we send mixed signals because:

- We were ignored the first (or first few) time(s)

- We want to keep you around but know we'll lose you once we put out

- We've been conditioned to hint, even though it doesn't work

- Sometimes we *don't* know what we want (don't play "I told you so"- neither do you if you're not one dimensional)

- We're afraid to actually express ourselves

- Everything's our fault (according to society)

- We overanalyze the shit out of everything (yeah, we do. Most of us own this).

- We *have* to be "paranoid" (actually, it's just safety)

- We have 8 million browser tabs open at once in our brains. All. The. Time.

- We've been conditioned to extremes

7.5 Why Women Seem to Go for Douchebags

So, you're hanging out with your friends, and the girl you like starts bitching about some douchebag who isn't treating her right. Again. As if you're not sitting *right fucking there.* Amirite?

So, you have to wonder, what the hell is wrong with me? Then you're like, nah. What the hell is wrong with her? I mean, I know she likes me. Why wouldn't she? And she knows I like her. I'm not exactly subtle. And the way she shifts *just so* when we're watching a movie- is she *trying* to feel for a boner, just to see if she's still got it? What the hell is she doing? She must know I can see right down her shirt from this angle. I'm trying not to look, but goddamn, what I wouldn't give to be suffocated by those. It would be a good death. Amirite?

Well, to start off, maybe. We do like to know we still got it. And you are kinda fun to tease. Because boobs. I mean, who doesn't like to know they still got it and play with boobies? Even gay men and straight women like them. But she's probably not actually *trying* to turn you on. Men are just super duper easy to turn on and hard as fuck to turn off. You got a chubby just reading that, didn't you? It's okay; I won't tell anyone.

But here's the rub (pun intended): Mr. Douchebag actually *told* her he liked her. He probably asked her on a real date or two. He gives her compliments without her fishing. Maybe he even dropped the L word (not *that* L word, the other one- the love word). He's pretty charming. We know charming is a red flag, but we like to be complimented and taken out on real dates and have guys go down on us without asking for it in return (are you taking notes? That one's huge). He says all the right things at exactly the right time. Feel free to break out into song again.

We're not stupid. We know you like us. We also know he's lying just to us just to get in our pants. But we believe him because we *want* to, not because we actually do.

And a part of us *really* doesn't want you to tell us how you feel. Then we have to either be honest and tell you we don't like you and we'll probably lose you as a friend, or we just won't give a straight answer and keep leading you on.

So why aren't we going for you, Mr. Nice Guy, Best Friend, in the first place? Let me lay it out for you.

- If you think you're a nice guy, you're probably actually not.

- If you think you're a douchebag, you probably actually are.

- Empirical evidence has trained us not to believe in nice guys.

- If you're being nice just to get laid, then whining about not getting laid, you're an incel, and the worst kind of douchebag there is.

- If you date your best friend, it can only go two directions, and most of us are scared of either.

- If you really are actually a legit nice guy, who doesn't expect sex for being a decent human being, I applaud you. And she's just not feeling it for whatever reason. Women can be shallow too. Or there's just no chemistry on her end. Don't force it. Love is like a fart. If you have to force it, it's probably shit.

But let's take the other approach. The one where you actually tell her how you feel. Try asking her on a real date. Use the word date. These are her options:

- Politely reject you and hope you're not a dick about it, ie, begging her to like you, whining, calling her names, going violent or stalkerish on her (all very valid fears)

- Politely reject you, and then ghost when you *do* become a dick about it

- Not so politely reject you

- Act crazy so you'll reject her

- Be vague and continue to lead you on

Or

- Say yes

I get that that's a scary path to take. It's scary for us too. But if you start off that conversation with openness and honesty, you'll most likely get rejected politely where she still legitimately wants to be friends and feels free from the burden of dangling sex, or she might say yes.

You'll never know until you try. Listen to the voice of experience here. Or lack thereof, which is almost as good. I never really stopped being afraid of commitment until *after* I was diagnosed with five chronic illnesses. Yeah, I wish I'd noticed that good guys existed before.

So, if you can handle rejection, you're already above most guys. Don't play the "friends until I can get into her pants" game. If you really can't do just friends, be like every other guy out there and ghost.

But if you really *can* do just friends, she's looking for the long haul. Not just a fuck. You have a better chance in the long game. She may someday become interested in you. Or you might meet someone through her. Or, get this, you both have an actual *real* friend you can open up to and be real with and don't have to hide who you are. So what if there's no romance there? They come and go. Real friends are forever.

Chapter 8

The "Friendzone"

On that note, there is "friendzone." What is that, the Phantom Zone? She either likes you or she doesn't. And if she wants to be "just friends," she doesn't like you.

I've been "friendzoned" a few times, and I've done it to guys. But no, I haven't, and I haven't. Because **it doesn't exist!** That's like saying you were stood up by Bigfoot. I guess, technically, we're all stood up by him every day. **Because he doesn't exist!**

Okay, lemme lay it out for you. Your guy friends- do you call them "friendzoned"? No, because they didn't hit on you. Your gay guy friends- are they "friendzoned"? No, because they knew hitting on you wouldn't go anywhere.

But the fat chick who likes you is friendzoned. Why? Because she had a real chance with you but you weren't interested? Then she never had a chance with you.

She can do just friends. She's not playing the "friends until I can get in his pants" game.

But listen up about the fat chick: *are* you actually interested in her but think you "deserve" a 10, and 10 means skinny, even-especially-if she's a psycho butterface?

Go for the 8's. Beauty fades. Crazy is forever. I really hope that's one of the three things you'll have memorized by the end. The other two are the cardinal rules.

Have you been friendzoned? Why do you think that? Because you had a real chance, and then she shot you down? Then you never had a real chance. Like your guy friends, like your gay guy friends, like your Nana's quilting mates who flirt with you because it's funny, and you flirt back because it's funny- there never *was* a real chance.

Which means, *you* never had a real chance if you've been "friendzoned," because it doesn't exist. There is no friendzone.

One guy got upset that I was using my *own* opinion to determine who I should sleep with. Ummm, who else's? My body, my choice. Clearly, he didn't treat me as a human being, so he didn't get laid. And he would've been just a fuck, too. Sometimes that's all we want too.

But we want it from someone who views us an entire human, not just tits and ass. We'll view you as an entire human if you want that. But I'm pretty sure many of you would be fine being just a cock.

You don't seem to realize how easy it is for us to get laid. We don't even have to try. Well, the ones who lack confidence have to try a *little.*

So, if we're not interested in you, we haven't banished you to the nonexistent friendzone. We're just not interested.

Chapter 9

Conclusion

Alright, let's do a quick summary of everything we've learned today, shall we?

Cardinal Rules

1. **Treat her like a human being**

2. **Back off when she says to**

Seriously, if you've got that, you're ahead of everyone else out there.

Mantra: Beauty fades, crazy is forever. Pick your battles wisely.

Quit overlooking the shy ones or the fat ones or, god forbid, the smart ones in favor of the Hollywood types with daddy issues.

What did we learn from Chapter One? There was a lot of good shit in there! It took one-third of the book!

But mostly, there are a lot of personality traits that are not inherent or genetic. You'll notice none of the what women want or don't want was based on physicality.

Men are attracted to what they see, and women are attracted to what they hear. That's why women wear makeup and men lie.

Shit, I wasn't gonna throw in any jokes. Now that I did, here's one more: why do women suck at parking? Because they've been lied to about what eight inches is too many times. I kill me!

Seriously, though, yes, of course there's an aspect of physical attraction, and everybody has a "type." There *has* to be attraction. But if she's not attracted to you, she's not attracted to you. Move on. Back away, not today.

Working on the *personality* traits will help you become a better man, and a better person. As they say, there's always more fish in the sea.

What did we learn from **Chapter Two**? Some of that was good, and some was bull's pizzle. Aren't you lucky to have clicked on a link written by a woman? Otherwise, you'd be stuck with that echo chamber of toxic masculinity and not know why you're striking out.

And yes, there's also toxic femininity, the kind where she feels entitled all the time and expects you to read her mind and gets upset when you can't, and *all* she can offer is that she's purty. This is your type, isn't it? <<insert bitchslap here>> Knock that shit off, man! She's gonna treat you like shit until the day you die! She's the kind to set your balls on fire if she finds another woman's number in your phone. Have I made myself clear yet? Say it again for the back row! **BEAUTY FADES! CRAZY IS FOREVER!**

What was **Chapter Three?** Oh, that's right, that was a whole avalanche of bullshit. Good thing you had me around to clear that up for you. The shit you've read written by men is all about tricking a woman to get her to sleep with you, then to continue tricking her to *keep* sleeping with you. Try honesty. It's a stretch, but it just might work.

Let's review **Chapter Four**. Set yourself apart from every other dude out there. Use the word "date." Plan it. Don't ask her to plan it. Don't ask her what she wants to do. She'll say "whatever," because she's already bored.

What did we learn in **Chapter Five?** This one threw me for a loop because it felt like the first four were setting you up to try to trick us into the sack, now you want a long-term relationship? Mind. Blown. Lemme help you out again. If you're tricking us to get laid, **don't** build a relationship on that. Just don't. Because for most women, no matter how badly you've fucked up, as long as you're honest, it can be worked out. Usually. One dude told me how he felt about another woman when it was in my mouth. I wish I'd bitten it. Don't be a dumbass, like that guy. Timing is essential, too.

But really, I was confused at this chapter. I was like, oh, it's *not* just about sex? Because everything I had to read in order to put in my own words and tell you what bullshit it was, was just about sex.

But you *do* want us for the long haul? **Then don't start off by tricking us to get us into the sack!!!!!**

Okay, are we clear on this chapter? Try honesty.

Alright, **Chapter Six.** Consent. Okay, chapters six on weren't in the original outline. I added them because I *do* know what women want. Yes, I've got the inside track, and it still took me the better part of thirty years to figure us out.

So, I get it that you don't. I really do. I also acknowledge that I'm fairly unique, being a guys' girl. Yes, I use the word there because it's the vernacular.

Other women don't "get" you as I do, but they certainly *get* you better than I do, if you catch my drift. Because they know how to play the game. I clearly don't. I just handed you our playbook. Hell, we're lucky I realize it *is* a game. I still handed you our playbook. Good thing my name isn't attached to this thing, huh?

Let's talk about consent. In the wake of **#metoo**, a lot of guys are freaked out that someone's gonna drag their name through the mud. Let me clarify a few things for you.

No woman, or person, for that matter, is emotionally prepared for the turmoil of accusing a man. Even the very, very, very few women who lie, end up biting off more than they can chew.

I'll tell my own story since no one knows me. I said yes. Absolutely. Then I said stop, you're hurting me. I said it three times. I guess he didn't hear me, even though I don't know how he couldn't. He chose not to. He didn't stop. I froze. I couldn't move until he was done. I was in a lot of pain. He was at such an angle, that when we got up, there was a lot of blood on my bed. I mean a lot. And I wasn't a virgin. And he wasn't that big. Just average. He was freaking out that he'd had sex with a woman on her period, which has consequences in his tribe. He didn't hear me tell him several times that I'd had a hysterectomy and I wasn't menstruating. Menstrual blood is a lot thinner and more watery than normal blood. Get used to knowing and respecting how a woman's body works. We're sick of how we're built and really have no choice over, being a constant source of shame. I went to the hospital in the morning because I still hurt so much. I had to have a surgery to repair the damage. And I *still* didn't realize it was rape because I'd said yes. But then I said stop. The friend who pointed out to me that it *was* rape also said I could've prevented it because it was only our second date. I couldn't have prevented it. Are you seeing my point? The friend who pointed out it *was* rape because I'd told him to stop, also suggested it was my fault. I lost her as a friend. She'd been a good friend. She kept me from being homeless after I became disabled because everyone becomes homeless if they become disabled. I guess I still was, but she kept me off the street. And I lost her when I came forward. The friend who pointed it out. And I lost another female friend. And the lead detective was a female, so he walked. And I still have PTSD from it. And I had to add that ER visit to the bankruptcy I filed for medical. Why would anyone put themselves through that mess if it weren't true?

My point is if you're worried that you're going to be accused, reevaluate your behavior. Get a verbal yes on everything. Stop when she says stop.

I wish my story were an isolated event. But I know that thousands, if not millions, of other people have a similar story.

This is why consent is important. Because *no one* understands it. We need more feminist men. Please, start trying to understand it. Stop blaming women. Stop brushing off other men's behavior as not a big deal.

Because in the grand scheme of things, my story is mild. It is *so* mild.

Anyway, that was a downer of a recap, but get consent. Onto **Chapter Seven.**

You're welcome. Yes, this is where I handed you our playbook. Use it wisely, grasshopper.

Chapter Eight. There is no fucking friendzone. She's just not interested!!!!

Bonus Track

Remember CD's, how there'd be a hidden bonus track like two full minutes after the last song, and it was always exciting because you always forgot it was there? This is your bonus track.

What Women Want (as written by an actual, live woman; don't listen to any other bullshit because it's bullshit)

We want actual conversation. We want real dates. We want you to listen to us the first time, whether we're saying "stop," or "please take out the trash." Most of us actually hate being nags.

It seems like we either have to be super passive or super bitchy like there's nothing in the middle. If you've read this far, I applaud you. I'm about to blow your.... mind. Yeah, in your wet dreams, pal. I'm actually on the passive side. Until I've said it a whole bunch and been completely invalidated every time. Then I get bitchy. Actually, that's pretty normal.

Dudes had to repeat *exactly* what I'd just said in grad school before it was considered an intelligent comment. Sometimes they were actually *trying* to give me the credit, but the profs were having none of it.

We want our voices to be heard. We want to be valued for our own inherent selves, as life itself, not as merely the vessel to another life.

We want what you guys want- stability, a roof over our heads, knowing where the next meal is coming from, knowing we can go to the doctor.

We want "our man" to be an equal, not another child we're raising. I quoted "our man" because we don't own you either.

We want compliments, and lots of them, but not so many that it feels like you're just trying to trick us into the sack again.

I'll give you a few pointers. **Never** mention weight. Even if it's to ask if she lost weight. Way too many women in this country are defined by their weight and conditioned to hate their bodies. I think it was out of sheer rebellion that I developed body confidence. Because if I were black or Latina or maybe even Asian (maybe), my curves would be sexy. But as I'm white, I'm supposed to hate them. But I don't. I kinda don't dig my body now, that it's stopped working. But I still don't hate it. It hates me. Grr.

But if you want to compliment her looks, make sure it's not upon meeting her, either online or in real life. There's a difference between being hit on and being harassed. If we don't know you, it's probably harassment. Again, the difference between a nice guy and a pervert is timing. The difference between harassment and a compliment is timing. But here are some examples of compliments.

Compliments about her looks that don't make you sound creepy:

- You look great!

- I love your eyes. They're beautiful. They really pop (or stand out or look great with) that color you're wearing.

- Your makeup is on point.

- Your hair looks really stylish. I hope you didn't go to too much trouble just for me. (Spoiler- if she likes you, she did. If she doesn't, she did it for herself. Either way, she'll say, "Oh, it was no trouble!" Follow up: "You just rolled out of bed like that? Wow, you're even more amazing than I thought!" Might make her smile.)

- Is that a new outfit? I love the style! (Even if you have no idea- say it enough, and you're bound to get it right eventually! But not too much or she'll catch on).

Compliments not about her looks:

- You're really good at <insert skill here>. Can you teach me? (Depending on how smart-assy your relationship is, here are a few examples):

  - Useless information on Taylor Swift.

  - Sounding smart. Damn, you've fooled me a time or two! (Make sure you're actually good friends first!)

  - Keeping pets alive. Except for your turtle. Rest In Peace, little dude.

  - Saving just enough cookie dough for like, two cookies. Who needs more than that anyway?

  - Laughing at all my lame jokes. I really appreciate it.

  - Having awesome pipe dreams!

  For anything real, and not smart-assy, you'll have to come up with that on your own. It might require you to pay attention.

- You're really smart.

- You do your job really well. I wish you were recognized more for it.

- You have an amazing singing voice.

- Your laugh is cute.

- I love the way you smile with your whole face!

Gift Suggestion Ideas:

- Bath & Body Works gift basket

- Chocolate or granola bar if she's one of those healthy freaks gift baskets (flower shops have more than just flowers)

- Gifts for her pet, which she loves more than you. Poor turtle. But not dog clothes, I mean, I get it when little dogs wear clothes because they already don't have dignity. But big dogs? Come on!

- Concert tickets (I'm still a little pissed I have to *pay* for a seat when I bring my own chair!)

- Gift certificates to a mechanic for oil changes and tire rotations (it's not just women who don't do this. I'd still have my truck if my guy friend who used it after I stopped walking had changed the oil. Like I nagged him to.)

- Books, movies. Again, look at her collection. Use her Amazon wishlist if she has one. If not, try to sneak her phone and look at her orders. Then take a few funny selfies. But don't change the language. Apparently, people hate when you do that, even if they've just drawn penises on your law books!

- Again, surreptitiously take a pic of her decor and/or bedspread and ask the female staff what would match that

- Gift certificates to her favorite hair salon, massage parlor, nail salon

- Gift certificates to her pet's groomer or credit at its vet (she still likes it more than you, but it's becoming a close call.)

- Can't really go wrong with flowers

Date Ideas on the Cheap:

- An actual dumpster. Hear me out. I once had a double date with a guy and his buddy and his date in an actual dumpster. The buddy's dad put them up for his job. The buddy had keys before it was used. The guys had set up a crappy card table and crates that they were going to throw away, and we ate off paper plates. Those bins are massive! Plus, it was a self-contained mess if they were going to kill us. Okay, not everyone has that option. Moving right along.

- A picnic on the roof. Picnics anywhere are fun, but be creative.

- Stargazing

- Making s'mores

- Inviting her over for a home cooked meal

- Movie in the park

- Dog walking

- Basketball

- Nerf gun fight. Loser cooks/ buys dinner. Let her pay for things occasionally.

- Poetry jam/ drum circle

- Church of a different religion than either of you

Okay, I've given you gift ideas and date ideas, and I've even given you our playbook. But here's the part you've really been wanting: what we want emotionally.

There is no "how to keep her" guide. If she's going to cheat, she's going to cheat. Just like no matter how amazing we are, if he cheats, it's not our fault (no matter what society says).

1. First and foremost, we want honesty. Again, it doesn't matter how badly you've fucked up, if you're honest, we can work it out. Honesty always. Not *after* you've been caught with your pants down. If you start off your relationship with honesty and continue never lying to her, you can work almost anything out. It'll vary from relationship to relationship, from woman to woman, but whatever can't be worked out when you've never lied to her, she'll probably wish she'd tried harder *to* work it out. Because all men lie. Or we expect them to, anyway because of empirical evidence.

2. Next, we want loyalty. Yes, you're going to be attracted to other women. We know this. We're also attracted to other men. Who you're attracted to *isn't* a choice, but who you sleep with *is*. It is more difficult for men to keep it in their pants than women. Again, empirical evidence. So don't put yourself in tempting situations. Don't go to strip clubs unless she's honestly cool with it. Actually, that's probably safe because it's just their *job*. They're not going to sleep with you. Don't make excuses to hang out with your attractive coworker. Don't call her your "work wife." It's just funny, and everybody does it, right? True. But the words we use, even-especially-in our common vernacular, carry a lot of weight.

Calling your attractive coworker your "work wife" may seem harmless, but you probably spend more time with her than your actual wife. You may never actually sleep with her, but the way you interact at work, you're emotionally cheating.

Emotionally cheating is so different from physically cheating. Because you don't actually *do* anything, you justify it as *not* cheating.

But do you look forward to seeing your "work wife" more than your actual wife? Do you find yourself laughing with her more, and fighting with your wife more?

What is she offering you that your real wife isn't? There is some kind of emotional void she's filling, even if you and your wife have a healthy sex life.

Do you guys walk in sync, swing your arms in sync? These are signals your subconscious is sending that you're a lot closer than you think.

Do you tell her your funny stories your wife is sick of? Do you find yourself making excuses to visit her cube? Do you go out to lunch nearly every day?

Do you laugh at the rumors swirling around the office because neither of you could ever cheat? But you *are* cheating. You're emotionally cheating.

Here are a few tips on how to spit shine your marriage. Again, why is a single person giving advice? One, I'm the perfect wife and will be until I get married. Perfect parent too. Until I adopt. Two, because I've seen a lot of marriages. In my geographical area, there's a huge divide between marrieds and singles. Bigger than in normal parts of the world, where it's already pretty big. Although childless marrieds are usually lumped into singles, and single parents have their own category no one knows what to do with. Really, they could just try treating them like human beings, but what do I know?

And I get it. Married people are on a different path than single people. Parents are on a different path than the childless. Whether single and/or childless is a choice, or whether it's been thrust upon you, you're on a different path.

But I've seen *a lot* of marriages. And divorces. And there is something to be said for the objective third party view. I'll have to find this and read this if I ever say yes. Or ask. But here are a few tips to spit shine your relationship, whether you're married or just starting to seriously date.

- Fill up your reservoir of funny stories/ happy memories/ good times. If your wife is sick of all your stories, ya gotta make more. You know how you get together with high school or college friends, and you relive the same ten or eleven memories and laugh like crazy, and you do this every five or six years? That's because you have a finite amount of memories with people you only see once or twice a decade.

Your wife, though, you should be making up more memories. You can't keep going through the same five memories from when you first started dating or she'll start bitching that you're not who you were when you started dating. And you've probably both changed at least a little. So fill up your reservoir of memories all the time. Keep making more funny and happy memories. Leave the house. When plans go tragically awry, don't wait ten years to find it funny. Laugh now.

- Give each other love notes often. More than just "I love you" or "butt stuff?" Real notes. What specifically do you love about her? Why did you marry her? Go through these notes after every fight, then make more.

- Find *something* to thank her for every day. If she's a stay at home mom, she's busier than you can imagine. But she's also more bored than you can imagine. Thank her for cleaning the kitchen, or making the bed, or taking care of the kids so you can work. If she burns dinner one night, let it go. Just thank her for it and eat it without complaint. I had a roommate who would eat all my experimental cooking without complaint, even the shit I wouldn't feed my dog. It was an amazing quality in a man. In anyone, really.

- Notice the little things that need doing around the house, and just *do* them. Men who do more housework get laid more often. Science. Even though you're an *actual* nice guy, and you're not doing it *to* get laid. Don't step over the pile of dirty clothes. Notice it. Put it in the wash. Change her oil. Notice the stuff around the house so that she *doesn't* give you a honey-do list. You live there too. And if you don't, but you still notice them and do them, without judgment, without yelling at her, just because you love her, she'll appreciate it even more.

- First, assume the other one means no harm. Have this discussion with her at the beginning- that you're a dude, and as such, you're gonna say a lot of dumb shit, and if anything can be taken in more than way, you meant it in the way that wasn't meant to hurt her. And when she overanalyzes, because she will, realize she's not trying to hurt you, either.

- Keep your fights to yourselves. This will require a frank and honest discussion at the onset of the relationship. People often tell friends the problems with their SO, but forget to tell them the cute things they do every day. She'll probably have a harder time than you with this. Make the compromise that if she doesn't tell her friends and family about your fights, you'll promise to open up to her. Because that's next on the list.

3. We want you to open up to us. Tell us about your dreams,

your hopes, your passions, your fears. Also, tell us about your day. Tell us enough about your work environment that we'll find Jerry's stupidity funny too. Ask us about our hopes, our dreams, our passions, our fears, our days. Don't rush in to fix a problem or tell her how to get her idea off the ground. Wait until she *asks* for you to fix her problems. And if you have ways how to get her ideas off the ground, ask her if she wants to really do it. Support if she says yes. But don't laugh at her dreams. Don't tell her they're unrealistic. That's why they're *dreams*. Just tell her about your unrealistic dreams.

4. We want discussions and communication. We need to be heard. We do a lot of shit we don't like just to make you happy, and I get that you guys do too. But if you give us more discussions, where our opinions are valid, and not wrong just because they're ours, we tend to fight less. If you listen to us when we talk, you won't have to hear us yell. So- more discussions = less fighting. More listening = less yelling. Most of us hate to yell. Especially at another adult. The kids are bad enough.

5. We want to be held and told everything's gonna be alright, even when things seem fine. We want you to let us do that for you, too. You don't always have to be the strong one. Because…

6. We want an actual partnership. You're not carrying us through all of life's storms, and we're not carrying you. We carry each other. Sometimes I fall and sometimes you do, and both are okay.

7. Lastly, we want to feel safe with you. Physically, emotionally, sexually, financially. We want to know our children are safe with you, physically, emotionally, sexually, financially. We may worry about if we can pay for the kids'

doctor bills, but we want to worry about that *together*. We don't ever want to have to wonder if you're coming home, or if you're cheating, or if you're going to hurt us in any manner. Maybe all the other ones have, and all of your exes hurt you, so the beginning will be tricky for both parties. But after we have that trust, we don't want it to **ever** be broken.

At the end of the day, we all want the same thing- to be heard, to be validated, to be loved.